WW II Germany —

ny. 1979. 172 p. Stated
1st ed. - f in f unclipt dj.

701

On the Other Side

BY RUTH EVANS

Happy Families: *Recollections of a Career in Social Work*

Mathilde Wolff-Mönckeberg

ON THE OTHER SIDE

To My Children: From Germany 1940-1945

Translated and edited by

Ruth Evans

MAYFLOWER BOOKS

Wolff-Mönckeberg, Mathilde
On the Other Side
ISBN 0 8317 6679 4

Manufactured in Great Britain
First American Edition

Contents

Illustrations

Illustrations Nos. 7, 8, 9 and 10 are reproduced by courtesy of the Imperial War Museum, London.

Foreword by Ruth Evans

Mathilde Wolff-Mönckeberg, my mother, who was always known as 'Tilli', was born on 1 April, 1879 in Hamburg. She was the seventh child and fifth daughter of Johann Georg Mönckeberg and Elise Mathilde (*née* Borberg-Tesdorpf), his wife. Elise Mathilde was of Swiss origin, while the Mönckeberg family had been resident in Hamburg since the middle of the eighteenth century, hailing originally from Westphalia.

I remember my grandmother. She was a minute, dainty little person who, after her husband's death in 1908, always wore black widow's weeds and a black crape bonnet with just a tiny white frill framing her face. She died when I was eight years old and I was the only granddaughter at that time who could wear her shoes, small narrow black pumps with just a thin strap buttoning around the ankle. Our relationship was not a close one, but then I was her thirty-fourth grandchild and had to share her affection with a host of others whom I barely knew. My mother, however, claimed a special bond of tenderness with her. Soon after Mathilde was born, the older children had scarlet fever and the baby Tilli had to be isolated. Nanny and nursemaids had their hands full looking after the sick-room and my grandmother took over the care of the youngest. Previously, social duties had not often allowed her to spend more than a rationed number of hours each day with her offspring; being a public figure of some consequence, my grandfather needed her by his side. My mother felt ever afterwards that this early intimacy marked a special tie between them.

Tilli grew up against the rather staid, traditional and somewhat exclusive rules of Hamburg society. Her father, as a busy lawyer and member of the City Council and Senate, regarded his parental duties as amply fulfilled by providing the wherewithal for his many children's education. Boys and girls alike were sent to excellent schools, had plenty of private tuition, and his four sons all had university careers of varying distinction. His daughters could pride themselves on mastering the gentle arts of music and painting, deportment and elocution, dancing and general social graces. The atmosphere was solidly and prosperously Victorian. But there was more. My grandmother's original background had been very unconventional, tinged with tragedy and early suffering. Her father, a

7

graduate and teacher at an educational establishment in Berne, had become an alcoholic and committed suicide by hanging himself in 1850, when she was only four years old. Her mother died very soon afterwards. The family was split up, Elise Mathilde Borberg was adopted by a Hamburg Senator and his wife, Herr and Frau Tesdorpf, a childless couple who took into their home and lives two small girls, totally unrelated, and brought them up as sisters. I do not know, nor have I ever heard, how this trauma affected her or what shadows it cast on her subsequent life. She was always described to me as serene and happy, outgoing and adaptable, but above all as somewhat unconventional for those days. She was very musical, had a remarkable pure soprano voice and when asked to sing would rise to any audience and any occasion without coyness or hesitation. What infiltrated into her children, and most of all perhaps into her youngest daughter, my mother, was undauntable courage; a gift to see the humorous side of life even in moments of darkest gloom; and a strong conviction in obeying the rules of society even if one had to bend them a little to fit particular sets of circumstances. I have no idea whether my grandmother's marriage was a happy one. There is more than one indication in her diaries that she found continuous childbearing burdensome. She gave the impression to the large family circle and even larger one of friends and acquaintances that she was contented; more than that, she enjoyed her children's talents, her husband's overall protection and the manifold opportunities for showing this off on occasions of stately entertainments. As Lord Mayor of Hamburg my grandfather had considerable status amongst the nobility of Germany, and my grandparents welcomed into their house a variety of royal and political personages, as well as musicians, poets and painters of international renown. I am myself not entirely unaffected when I read in Grandmother's notebook : 'Fürst Bismarck for lunch. Herr Johannes Brahms for dinner.' And yet I feel she took it in her stride.

I have, in beautiful copperplate Gothic script handwriting, a diary kept by my mother in the year 1892, when she was thirteen years old. She records in great detail her parents' Silver Wedding. My grandfather's gift to his silver bride was a painting by Gottfried Hofer of the whole family with Fürst Bismarck as guest of honour in the middle. 'Monday 6th June,' she writes, 'I rose early. Walking downstairs I saw him— [Gottfried Hofer, obviously the object of much girlish adoration]. My pulses raced in excitement, it was heavenly. My governess was there too, little Fräulein Möller. Soon more people arrived and when our parents appeared, Herr Hofer wanted to efface himself and disappear. The staircase was decorated with fresh green branches. We nine children stood in a row. It was a grand moment and a triumphal procession entered the big drawing-room. Hofer's picture was a tremendous surprise. A note from him was affixed to it : "This sketch is to anticipate the painting Hofer will create." Oh, if only I could imitate his handwriting ! Gratitude spilled over, Papa expressed his thanks with dignity, Mama tenderly, and he bent over her hand and kissed it. Big pearls of tears were in the artist's eyes. Then he left. Adolf and Franz [her younger brothers] recited their poem, and when Adolf finished with "love reigns eternal" everybody sobbed, deeply moved. At breakfast Papa read a psalm, his voice faltered and there were tears in his eyes. When my sister Mimi said the Lord's Prayer she could not continue, lowered her head and cried. Suddenly all the domestic staff came in to offer their felicitations with so much heartfelt appreciation that one could not but feel in what esteem they hold my parents. And after breakfast visitors started to arrive, a never-ending stream of them. At 11.30 the town band came to serenade them. When they played the wedding march, my heart nearly burst with bliss. I could not take my eyes off my beloved parents. Huge baskets and bouquets of flowers were brought, over eighty of them. In between a hasty lunch, and then we had more callers, well over two hundred in all, and all our reception rooms were full to bursting. We had a terrific time, giggled and laughed and rushed around. He, the wonderful man, also came with his enchanting wife. The more I notice that I really mean nothing to him, that I am just another young girl, the bigger my love for him grows. I burn and tremble for him, who is my all. I shall never marry, will devote my whole life to my adored parents. I will never be able to love anybody as I love "him", never, never. Then we had a little rest before changing. The evening was spent with Mama's sister Tante Olga Des Arts. When we arrived a fanfare was played. Mama looked gorgeous, so dainty and sweet, the truest and most beautiful little silver bride. Papa was so distinguished and stately, an imposing silver groom. We young ones sat round a smaller table. There were at least twenty toasts, and cousin Lili and I had dreadful attacks of gigglishness, horrid really and quite undignified, but we were in a foolish mood. There was lovely table music, the band played all our favourite tunes. Best of all our sweet grandmama was with us, surrounded by all her dear ones. The whole garden was lit up with paper lanterns right down to the Alster. One could hear all the melancholy and boisterous tunes drifting across the trees. Lili and I walked arm in arm; every now and again, according to the music, we danced and galloped madly; then again we would just whisper to each other about our secret loves, and we finally came to the conclusion that only Jesus is the true friend of one's soul. Then stupid Heini disturbed us, tried to pay court to Lili. We nearly died laughing and paid no attention. When we got home I fairly fell into bed, but oh so contentedly. Such a Silver Wedding cannot ever be repeated, heart my heart do not ever forget this.'

Tilli finished her schooling at sixteen and had by that time acquired a very considerable fluency in French and English, was a passable pianist and quite an accomplished singer, treading in the footsteps of her sisters, who by this time had 'come out', two of them being married, the other two engaged. She was sent to a finishing school in Eisenach before being launched as a fully-fledged débutante on Hamburg society. There were parties and balls, picnics and excursions, and a remarkable succession of young gentlemen, eligible and well brought up, who sought her favours and her father's consent to pay court to her. There was a deep and lasting attachment to her older brother Carl, but also a growing feeling of restlessness and discontent. On 23 August, 1899 she writes : 'I am committing one folly after another, I have really got to pull myself together. There seems very little point in anything and my intellect is slowly drying up. I am attuned only to physical pleasures, my thoughts are poisonous and I cannot get any help from concentrating on worthwhile work. I'm trying to help Franz with his piano practice, but think only of my own past. Ten proposals of marriage in three years, between the ages of seventeen and twenty, an average of three per year. How crazy ! I'm icy cold writing this down and yet there were moments when I was anything but cold. And there is always this dreadful longing for something different.'

Much to my grandparents' surprise and not inconsiderable chagrin, Tilli begged to be allowed to go to Italy to study Italian and singing. This took a lot of arranging, but they were wise enough to let her go with their full consent and blessing. I would guess that my grandmother's part in this decision was one of understanding diplomacy and a certain amount of wheedling as far as the stern Bürgermeister was concerned. Chaperons were needed, reliable friends to keep an eye on Tilli, and they were found in the art historian Dr Aby Warburg and his wife who were at that time living in Florence. The friendship with this family has now reached the fourth generation, never varying in its degree of intensity and intimacy. Tilli left Hamburg in late October 1899, not to return for any length of time until after World War I. As was to be foreseen, a young girl who had lived such a sheltered life was bound to be homesick. In fact her early daily letters are pathetic outcries of loneliness. 'Do not think, my dearest Mama, that I am not grateful for your unbelievable kindness and generosity. But I cannot but confess to you, my own Mother, that I am unable to find it in me to laugh myself out of this frightful desolation, and every garment I take out of my trunk is watered by my tears in the realization that I have to do without your caring love. I have, I'm afraid, a very weak character.' Having changed her original lodgings much against Dr Warburg's advice, she writes to her father very soon afterwards in November 1899 : 'The Warburgs are happy that I am more settled and I am a constant guest in their house. They fulfil all my ideals of a married couple, share the same interests and tastes, co-operate in all their endeavours and function in complete harmony. Last night I went to have dinner with them and their great friend, a young Dutch art historian, called Jolles, escorted me back to the Pensione, where he too is lodging.'

This then is the first mention of Tilli's future husband, my father, André Jolles. Their attachment progressed very quickly and on 25 December, 1899, Tilli, in a very long letter to her mother, writes : 'May I, my darling Mama, inform you of the biggest Christmas wish I have, imploring you at the same time not to pass this on to anybody? I wish with all my heart and soul that you will bestow upon me your utmost trust – both you and Papa – and that you could prepare yourself to like and trust André Jolles. Nothing you would not approve of will happen until you come on your promised visit to Florence in spring. But if then he tells you that he loves me and that we cannot live without each other, please do believe him. We have lived through days of great heartsearching and most serious deliberations, and believe me, Mama, this time I did not just raise a little finger and he came. There was another lady involved who was devoted to him, but he loves me. We have told Dr and Mrs Warburg and they reiterated that no final word must be spoken until you come, until you can see for yourself that this time everything is completely different, that we would not do anything without your consent and will wait for your permission to get engaged. Oh Mama, I hope you will love him. He is not an easy character and one has to love him very profoundly to make him happy.' And a couple of days later : 'Jolles is not an easy person to understand. It is not just his intelligence which I find so impressive. He is a mixture of earnestness and almost childish fun. It is not just one thing alone, it is the whole of him I hold in such loving esteem, also that I feel he needs me. This ultimate wish of wanting to be together through thick and thin, makes me believe that we belong to each other. – Since his father died, when André was only a child, he has always lived with his mother in Amsterdam. She is a writer of some standing and leads a circle of poets and artists. During his father's illness she devoted herself entirely to nursing him, such a strain that it left her with a nervous skin condition. At times this becomes so acute and harassing that she suffers dreadfully. At this very moment she is in hospital. Dr Warburg says she is one of the finest and most sensitive women he has ever met. He always talks of little Mama Jolles. Unfortunately she hardly speaks any German. André, her only child, is loved and spoilt by her and no one will ever take his place in her life. He belongs to the type of human beings who will need in perpetuity to have a person or persons who give their entire attention to him and to his work, who will encourage and refresh him during times of melancholy and despondency. Is it not like a miracle to be chosen to help such a man who has the highest attributes of intellect? And does he not bestow all his confidence in me? I no longer need any books, he answers all my queries; he demands co-operation from me and has piled up such a vast programme of work for me that life will never be dull again. I am completely convinced that I have reached a goal after so many false starts, that I have found happiness and that life is kind and good. No longer the torturing question : What is it all about? which haunted me when I left Hamburg and arrived in Florence. I know my behaviour has worried you in the past. Could there have been a better answer than this? Sweetest little Mama, perhaps I'm not all bad and useless after all.'

This unconventional beginning to Tilli's courtship and married life could only be rectified in the eyes of the wider family and Hamburg society by an ultra-traditional wedding in due course. Suspicion that this curious match would not last never entirely left some members of her former circle. The originality of André Jolles' mind, his artistic and academic output nevertheless swept many people off their feet, and he undoubtedly became a strong influence on members of my mother's family as well as on many other passers-by on their way through matrimony.

After their marriage in September 1900 Tilli and André settled in Italy, having bought a small Strozzi villa in San Domenico, outside Florence. In June 1901 their first child was born, a boy, Hendrik Jolle, who died tragically of gastro-enteritis a little over a year later in July 1902. The young couple was defenceless against this relentless stroke of fate. Throughout her long life Tilli never fully recovered from this loss which, for a long time, seemed to her like a judgement on the follies of her inconsiderate youth. They fled, leaving behind them many of the collected treasures of their early life together.

Much later my mother wrote in some fragmentary reminiscences : 'After our heartrending experiences we bade farewell to our beloved home, and to the small grave in the *cimitero* in San Domenico, where in unconsecrated ground on the pathway our small son was buried, accompanied on this last stage of his journey only by us and the gardener Tonino who carried the coffin. Only one wreath from Tonino and Adelia, our maid. *"Al nostro caro Signorino in signia dei grata memoria."* My thoughts go on to Freiburg, that charming little town in South Germany, surrounded by hills and woods, which gave us such a friendly welcome and brought many a new friendship. Life carried on, and like collectors, we accumulated a fresh circle around us. The unknown little student from Holland completed his degree and became one of the most popular academic lecturers. Doors were thrown open for him and everybody recognized and admired his versatile and brilliant mind, his attractive personality. Not only his lectures and tutorials, but also his colourful imaginative gifts, his work as producer and designer were immensely popular, and no party or performance would be arranged without his assistance. People were talking about "Jollesianismus"; he went so far as to accompany ladies to their dressmaker to influence their taste, and I was regarded as the best-dressed woman in society. I gave a solo dance display, played the title-role in his drama "Alceste", translated his books and pamphlets [he continued to write in Dutch], attempted to become a poetess in my own right, and in vanity and self-righteousness succumbed to acts of foolishness and transgression. Our common anchor were the three children, our three lovely children. But André resented the tie, pulled up his roots once more and left. The Freiburg dream was ended.

'Again it was flight really. Only this time it was not death that drove us away but our lack of self-discipline, involvements in confused personal relationships which could be resolved only by abdication. He first, then we all moved to Wannsee, near Berlin, our new domicile. I went with very mixed feelings, my heart was torn between despair and new hope. Perhaps all would be well in the end. I had my three children and nothing would ever make me part from them. I also had darling faithful Mimi, who had joined the family when my eldest daughter was born and stayed as my prop and helpmeet through years of trials and tribulations. She came with us into the new large and dignified house, which was situated in the shade of mighty fir-trees on the shady soil of

Northern Germany. Nothing was as light and friendly and comfortable as my beloved home in Freiburg. I never became as fond
of Wannsee as I had been of Baden. As usual André was lucky. No
sooner had he arrived, than he found plenty of people who were
interested in his work and he was offered a post at the Institute of
Education in Berlin. He took a further degree at Berlin University
and put out feelers for further research and teaching. Around us in
Wannsee we had a colony of artists, art historians and art
designers, technicians and executants who formed a lively group of
interchanging ideas. The children found playmates, later on school-
mates, and shared in a privately founded school. We were not short
of anything. André loved the accelerated speed of life in Berlin, the
hubbub of the Friedrichstrasse, where the Institute was situated,
gave himself entirely to the busy metropolis and did not look back
with any nostalgia to our once simple and peaceful existence in
Freiburg. I always felt a bit of an outsider, almost a stranger, in
Wannsee. My women companions here were no dilettantes in their
artistic aspirations or intellectual pursuits and with a sure instinct
sensed that my playful tendencies made me feel only a primitive
kind of female rival with no intrinsic value or talents of her own.*
Beneath those rather forbidding and dark fir-trees I longed for
colour and flowers, also for the superficial but attractive interplay
of the Freiburg circle. The most blissful moment during our time
in Wannsee was the birth of our third son [Matthijs]. This truly
forged a new strong link between André and me, we both wanted
this our fifth child very much indeed and he brought us much mutual
happiness. My two younger brothers were constant companions in
our home; both very musical, they brought a new dimension of
enjoyment to our midst. I was made to accompany Adolf, who was
a fine singer, and often trembled with nervousness. Again I was
persuaded to do some solo dancing before a critical audience in the
Institute of Art and Design. There were indeed plenty of excitements, and meanwhile our three children grew up and fat little
Thys became a curly blond favourite with everybody. André
always had a special and proud preference for his two daughters.
Jan, the third [child], was a dreamy inward-looking little boy,
totally different from his father who always treated him contemp-

---

*This remark, that she had 'no talents of her own', is very far from the
truth. Earlier she mentions that she translated André Jolles' books and
pamphlets; she became a skilled translator from both Dutch and Italian into
German. I still possess her translation of J. Huizinga's *The Waning of the
Middle Ages,* published in German (*Herbst des Mittelalters*) in 1923.

tuously and harshly, which led to many altercations between André
and me. Jan was tied intensely to me and I felt a deep understanding for him. When in 1914 I was expecting my last and youngest
child, war broke out. Again André felt compelled to take flight,
compelled to change his nationality and become a German citizen,
compelled to enlist as a private soldier and to follow the thousands
of others who were streaming towards the French frontier. He was
far away when baby Ruth was born, far away in more than one
sense, and our marriage finally tore apart. Little Ruth, the war
child, was my comfort.

'With my five children I returned to Hamburg in 1917, without a
husband and badly bruised by circumstances and fate. Yet still I
had not learned my full lesson of self-discipline, was prey to temp-
tations and faltered on many a threshold of responsibility. I was
aware that the break-up of my marriage was as much my fault as
his, that we both had taken far too many things for granted including creature comforts and financial security. How lucky I was to
find a new setting, securer and more peaceful love, I did not fully
realize until much later.'

In 1925 Tilli married Emil Wolff, who was born and bred in
Munich. His father, a stockbroker, had died; his mother and un-
married sister Ida lived in Munich, the latter being a dedicated and
hard-working social worker. Both Tilli and Wolff, as he was always
known to us, were forty-six years old and she brought into this
new union her five more or less grown-up children. He must have
been very much in love with her and a very courageous man to
boot, for he was a bachelor and had thus far lived exclusively for
his studies. André Jolles was by this time Professor of Comparative
Languages, Dutch and Flemish at Leipzig University, had remarried and had three further children. Emil Wolff was Professor
of English Language and Literature at Hamburg University.
Strangely enough, he and André had met during the war when
both were lecturing temporarily at Ghent in Belgium. It was there
that Tilli met Emil Wolff for the first time. Despite all her self-
confessed superficial extravagances and attractive vagaries, my
mother was essentially a deeply faithful person. Whoever had once
belonged to her life, stayed in it. She never lost interest in and
affection for André, kept in touch with him and his much younger
second wife for many years, and they met occasionally.

By mutual consent, Tilli's three older children, Jella, Jacoba and
Jan, spent a lot of time during the post First World War years in
Leipzig, while André paid maintenance for my brother Thys and
myself, who remained almost exclusively with her. This ceased

when she remarried. For reasons best known to my parents I never spent any time with my natural father except for one short holiday in 1930 when he took me to Holland. It was not a success and I never saw him again. My personal affections were and always will be strongly engaged with my stepfather.

After the grim years of poverty caused by inflation and the general post-1918 dilemma in Germany which overshadowed my childhood, we emerged into a much brighter period after my mother remarried. My grandmother had died in 1923. She had been perhaps unduly distressed by Tilli's and André's divorce. It was yet another blow in a world already shattered by the war, which had torn apart the life-long security and well-accustomed stability of her existence. The rest of Tilli's family kept somewhat aloof. I well remember the staunch but also rigid attitude of Hamburg society : there are certain things one does not do, and if one does do them, one at least does not talk about them. Of course Tilli was accepted back into their midst, after all she was a Mönckeberg, but . . . and there were quite a number of 'buts'. Perhaps significantly it was at this time that Tilli hyphenated her surname and added it to her maiden-name, a practice she continued for the rest of her life. What may have started as a compromise became an unquestioned prerogative. It is in fact a common occurrence in Holland for a woman to use and hyphenate both her names, but up till then Tilli had not done this. How different we all were from our Hamburg relations was related to me much later by one of my aunts. They had a saying : 'What in other children is regarded as disobedience and naughtiness, is called "originality" in the Jolles children !'

And yet the imperturbable regard for the fitness of things, the traditional belief in a rather unimaginative continuity, the conservative view of progress within prescribed and well-established limits gave the patrician inhabitants of the old Hamburg, the free Hanse city, their strength and in many ways their uniqueness. Much of this was accepted, bred into my mother. Much of it she constantly spurned and tried to discard, causing herself pain and leading to harsh self-criticism. Hitler's new Reich heightened Hamburg's superior attitude for a while. Without doubt or question, Jewish citizens had always been fully accepted members of all the town stood for, of its administration, of its commercial and artistic endeavours and accomplishments. The dignity of the prosperous and exclusive families, Jewish and Gentile alike, was offended by the 'common little house-painter from Austria' whose satanic powers were brushed aside, and whose not entirely *comme il faut* behaviour found only derisive disregard. But down by the harbour were also strange groups of militant leftists, a strong Communist element which slowly but surely infiltrated into the ranks of the young intellectuals, artisans and students. Hamburg conservatism almost nursed this subversive movement because it kept Hitler at bay. No wonder he refused to make more than one of his early flamboyant speeches in Hamburg, having missed his accustomed hysterical welcome and acclaim and being subjected to outspoken antagonism when he ventured into the city. All this was of course before the fateful year of 1933. After Hitler's accession to power there was less open criticism, less outspoken disgust, less fearless negation. Some of the dowagers began to admire Hitler's blue eyes and his tidy uniform. Perhaps he wasn't such a bad chap after all. Businessmen were impressed by the decline in unemployment, by the greater punctuality of rail and sea travel, by cheaper commodities for daily use. Political enemies of the régime went underground.

My father André Jolles joined the National Socialist Party in 1933 and became a convinced and ardent supporter of Adolf Hitler. He cut off all his former associations which did not lie in the same direction.

My stepfather Emil Wolff, despite considerable pressure, never became a member of the party and for better or for worse stuck to his firm belief that on the other side of this grim hell, real values would be found again only if one never ceased to have faith in them. I was far too immature to find my own way unaided through these labyrinthine extremes, and had I grown up with the one rather than the other, the course of my future life might have been very different.

Tilli had to prepare herself for and adapt herself to inevitable separations, separations from us children who were always nearest to her heart. My brother Jan had already left us in 1924. He perhaps as much as anyone had suffered from the breakdown of the marriage; he had been unsettled and restless, drifting from one occupation to another, and was still unnecessarily chastised – for what? – by my father's contempt. He emigrated via Holland to South America where, in due course, he devoted himself whole-heartedly to the Communist Party. He married Antonia Banegas, a girl from the Argentine, and had two sons, who, according to tradition, were given family names. He returned briefly to Hamburg in 1933, having been deported as a Communist agent. It remains a miracle to this day that, being landed in Nazi Germany, he remained unmolested for a number of weeks and managed to

cross over into Russian territory. He stayed in Russia for further
political training and then went back to South America. We never
saw him again. He died in Ecuador in 1942. My eldest sister Jella
became the wife of Hellmuth Goldschmidt. They had both studied
engineering but she did not complete her course. They lived first in
Breslau, my brother-in-law's home town, and then in Frankfurt
o.M. but left Germany for good in 1937, when it became all but
impossible for a half-Jewish family to live a normal unthreatened
life in the Reich. They settled in Denmark, but fled to Sweden
during the war, when Denmark was occupied by German troops.
My brother Thys, having taken a degree at Heidelberg University
and absolved his military service, went via England to the United
States of America in 1938. He married Hermione Reynolds, an
English girl. In the same year I married a Welshman, Ifor Evans,
and went to live in Aberystwyth. So of Tilli's five children only
Jacoba was left. Jacoba and her husband Gustav Heinrich Hahn,
both medical doctors, stayed in Hamburg and supported my
mother and my stepfather.

Tilli's second marriage was a happy one, although she never
found the haven of security which at times her imagination conjured up for her. Outward circumstances denied stability; her
self-questioning mind provided no escape; and her intense desire
to research into all the recesses of existence, to understand, to hold
and to incorporate all she found into her life and into her relationships with us, her children, be it pain or joy, gave her little peace.
Yet more than anybody I have ever known, she remained young in
spirit. She had a capacity for enjoying herself which was hugely
infectious, and in moments of delight the grass was never greener
on the other side of the hill. This happy trait was shared by Tilli's
faithful companion throughout the vicissitudes of her life : Mimi,
our nurse, protector and general factotum. Mimi joined the family
after the tragic death of Tilli's eldest child, Hendrik, and before
the birth of Jeltje, and she never left us until shortly before her
own death, at the age of eighty-two, in 1944. For over forty years
Mimi watched over and cared for us, loved and stood by Tilli
and her children.

Mimi – her full name was Marie Kleinmagd – was born and bred
in a tiny place in the Black Forest. She was of sound, honest
peasant stock and her people farmed a small piece of land, kept a
few animals at the outskirts of a hamlet three or four miles from
Freiburg im Breisgau. Early in her life she went into domestic
service, learned a little French in Alsace Lorraine and acquired all
the skills of house- and parlour-maid, cook and children's nanny,

which were to prove indispensable to the young and inexperienced Tilli. In fact she took over the household of the youthful Jolles couple and, although not at first entrusted with the care of the new baby, she soon became irreplaceable in every region of household duty. Tilli's children turned to her as to the very source of affection and unalterable sympathy. Small and slender, she was tough and energetic and her lap the best refuge for a child in trouble. There was never any rivalry between mistress and servant. They giggled together like young girls, but Mimi always knew instinctively when to call a halt to such intimacy. They also quarrelled and at times a veritable holocaust of disagreement would break out between them, the force of their passionate individual tempers all but sweeping them asunder. But always they found their way back into each other's confidence through their shared love for us and their similar sense of humour. Unlike my mother, however, Mimi was able to suffer fools gladly, not from lack of intelligence or insight, which she possessed to a high degree, but by simple faith. She did not scatter her love, but in those on whom she bestowed it she could perceive no faults. If they were irritating or unjust, she made excuses and forgave. The path these two women travelled together was not smooth, but they supported each other and neither could have faced two world wars as bravely and patiently without the companionship of the other.

During the 1930s the circle of Tilli's family and friends began to disintegrate, at first surreptitiously, then with accelerated haste. A new element of pseudo-sociological thinking and racial consciousness infiltrated and insinuated its way into society, perceptible initially as a mere nibbling at the corners, a secretive but smug confidence in people who had never previously appeared to be interested in anything but their own careers and comforts. One became aware of sharply dissenting political views and of rapaciously growing prejudices. Looking back, it still seems almost miraculous that public servants like Emil Wolff carried on unmolested and uncurbed; that his method of teaching was regarded as a harmless aside, as old-fashioned liberalism and no immediate threat to the growing indoctrination elsewhere. His subtleties were probably too subtle to be noticed. And his did become a rather withdrawn existence. Marching, saluting and shouting were foreign to his taste and inclinations. Tilli was far more given to boisterous outbursts and sometimes shocked him with her fearless denunciations of what she regarded as vulgar and inappropriate. But he had no less courage; he took my brother Jan unquestioningly into his house, when many people thought this a very risky thing to do. Nor did he ever deny his profound allegiance to moral, academic and artistic values then discredited, and he pursued a unique path of honesty through bitter years of darkness and discord.

Tilli still had much of her early upbringing in her; not for nothing did my brother-in-law Gustav call her 'The Hamburg State Princess'. While the vicious storm gathered more momentum than was realized or recognized abroad, particularly in Great Britain, Hamburg still stood somewhat aloof, resting on its commendable laurels of a long history of independence, foreign trade and worldwide connections. It was not predominantly an intellectual or academic centre, but a port, a trading centre, one of the greatest in the world. Its post First World War University was still rather a novelty and was seen by many as an almost unnecessary enrichment. Once, at a formal gathering in the town hall, Tilli was accosted by a formidable lady who asked delicately, but with ungovernable curiosity : 'What is it like to be married twice running to a professor? I suppose it must be quite interesting.'

When, in 1938, my husband and I came for our last visit to Nazi Germany – our first and only one as a married couple – we were surprised to experience so little of what we expected to find in the way of crazy hotbeds of intrigue, deprivations and threats of violence. The affluent and outgoing society which received us might have been very misleading had there not been gaps in our circle of friends and relations, people who had either emigrated or had disappeared into concentration camps.

In the spring of 1939, Tilli returned our visit, coming to stay with us in Aberystwyth. She was well aware of the gathering clouds on Germany's horizon. As for many of her contemporaries, the 1914-1918 War had so drastically severed one period of her life from another, had so mutilated ideals of freedom and cohesion that Tilli feared nothing so much as a repetition. That for a second time this kind of disaster should overtake her was, in 1939, almost more than she could bear. And this time four of her five children were, so to speak, 'on the other side', out of her reach. During her visit we took her on a journey through South Wales and the South of England and saw her off at Dover. My husband and I stood for a long time on the quayside after the ferry had left and the white speck of her handkerchief had disappeared. We did not speak, but each knew what was in the other's mind.

Tilli Wolff-Mönckeberg's letters which follow were written to us, her children, during that endless spell of suffering and isolation. I know that these monologues were more than a necessity for her, that they became a lifeline and also a testament. Deep down she was convinced that she would not survive, and she could not leave us without these statements of harsh and at times even trivial facts, and without this bequest of her love. She did survive, however, and it is typical of her that, once released from the bondage of war, she put aside this document of diary letters and probably never thought of it again. Certainly she never mentioned it to me. Many of her accounts of events in Hamburg between 1939 and 1946 were repeated in post-war letters and during subsequent happy reunions.

I found this manuscript only five years ago when, in the cellar of my sister Jacoba's house, I was sorting through the contents of an old Italian settle from the flat at Andreasstrasse 39, where my mother and stepfather had lived throughout the war. At the very bottom, pushed right out of sight, was a big yellow envelope, battered and frayed at the edges. It contained these letters. The paper bears witness to the deterioration of writing materials; every inch of the scarce commodity is filled and the original text is divided only by dates : there are no paragraphs. Towards the end the ink becomes paler and less legible, the words more hieroglyphical. One can see by the curled corners and torn pages that the manuscript had been handled hastily, probably stuffed many times into an already over-full suitcase as the siren announced another air raid. Four more careful hands could not have smoothed and straightened those pages that day than Jacoba's and mine.

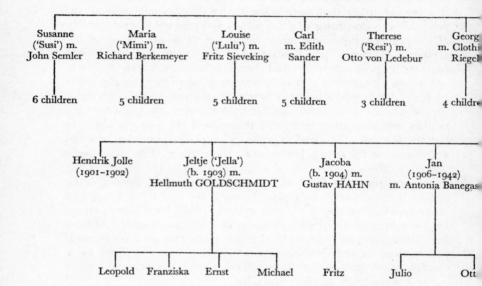

Johann Georg MÖNCKEBE[RG]
(1838–1908)

Susanne ('Susi') m. John Semler	Maria ('Mimi') m. Richard Berkemeyer	Louise ('Lulu') m. Fritz Sieveking	Carl m. Edith Sander	Therese ('Resi') m. Otto von Ledebur	Georg m. Cloth[i] Riegel
6 children	5 children	5 children	5 children	3 children	4 childr[en]

Hendrik Jolle
(1901–1902)

Jeltje ('Jella')
(b. 1903) m.
Hellmuth GOLDSCHMIDT

Jacoba
(b. 1904) m.
Gustav HAHN

Jan
(1906–1942)
m. Antonia Banega[s]

Leopold   Franziska   Ernst   Michael   Fritz   Julio   Ott[o]

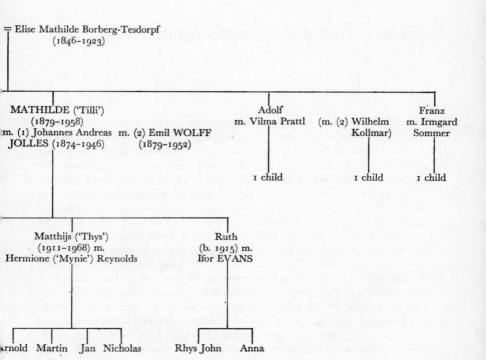

= Elise Mathilde Borberg-Tesdorpf
(1846–1923)

MATHILDE ('Tilli')   Adolf   Franz
(1879–1958)   m. Vilma Prattl   (m. (2) Wilhelm   m. Irmgard
m. (1) Johannes Andreas   m. (2) Emil WOLFF   Kollmar)   Sommer
JOLLES (1874–1946)   (1879–1952)

                                           1 child   1 child   1 child

Matthijs ('Thys')   Ruth
(1911–1968) m.   (b. 1915) m.
Hermione ('Mynie') Reynolds   Ifor EVANS

Arnold   Martin   Jan   Nicholas   Rhys John   Anna

Editor's Note and Acknowledgments

On the Other Side is an intensely personal work, written in circumstances of discomfort and physical danger. For news of the outside world Mathilde Wolff-Mönckeberg was dependent upon newspaper reports, radio bulletins and hearsay, and the information she presents in her pages inevitably differs on occasion from that of later historians writing with the benefit of official documents and hindsight. It would have been pedantic and tedious to correct or annotate each minor 'innacuracy' in dates or statistics, and with the exception of a very few instances where I have added footnotes to correct or illuminate her text, deleted the occasional repetitious sentence, or provided information identifying the persons referred to, Mathilde Wolff-Mönckeberg's manuscript is presented here as it was written. The original, handwritten manuscript has no paragraphs; those in the printed text were therefore created by myself.

I should like to thank my two sisters, Jeltje Goldschmidt and Jacoba Hahn, and my sister-in-law Hermione Jolles for their support and encouragement. My thanks are also due to Mrs Frede Prag (*née* Warburg) and Miss Barbara Sturgis for their invaluable help with the translation. Any errors are of course mine alone.

Oxford, 1978   R.E.

On the Other Side

Wie? Wann? und Wo? – Die Götter bleiben stumm!
Du halte dich ans Weil, und frage nicht Warum?

GOETHE, *Lyrische Dichtungen, Weimar 1810–12*

10 October, 1940.

My beloved far-away children, everything I was not able to tell you in my letters during the first year of the war, was not *allowed* to say, because the censor waited only for an incautious word in order to stop a message from getting through to you, all this I will now put down on paper under the title 'Letters that never reached them'; so that much later perhaps you will know what really happened, what we really felt like and why I had to reassure you repeatedly that the 'organization' was marvellous, that we were in the best of health and full of confidence.

It was completely different and very strange. When on 1 September, 1939, war broke out, your stepfather Wolff and I and all those nearest to us were in absolute despair. We were convinced that immediate and total annihilation would follow, and we had one thought alone : what can I do? where can I help? Anything rather than just sitting and waiting. Personally I could not understand why W[olff]. had periods of passive depression. I urged him to offer his services and we often quarrelled. I wanted to learn nursing, but your sister Jacoba* vetoed this, and consequently, in my inactivity, I was prey to torturing impressions of insane events. War, so the newspaper, the radio and many people proclaimed, was to be let loose again, war which meant to me the vilest of crimes against humanity; and this time it would be far worse than in 1914. This war would be conducted with the most horrible weapons and resources, its whole justification based on a daily incitement of lies, not an honest war, but an illegal and mean exploitation, as far as we were concerned.

The baiting, persecution and expulsion of the Jews had inflamed all decent people with anger and had created enemies for us. Now we [the German people] were to believe that in our innocence we had been wantonly attacked, that our own exertions to maintain peace had been obstructed, that we were being forced

---

*Jacoba Hahn, Mathilde Wolff-Mönckeberg's second daughter and her only child still living in Germany in 1939.

to take up arms. Many agreed enthusiastically with this false interpretation of events. *We* had stretched out the hand of peace; *we* wanted only Europe's salvation. But we were being cheated out of our good intentions, discredited by lying neighbours and all we could do was to fight back. In truth this whole campaign had been planned long ago, the Führer's blind lust for conquest, his megalomania being the driving forces behind the deed. For me nothing was more devastating than the fact that nobody, not even those who opposed the régime most vehemently, stood up against this, but remained passive and weak. I cannot stress these facts too strongly. It was as if we were caught in a stranglehold. And, worst of all, one even gets used to being half throttled; what at first appeared to be unbearable pressure becomes a habit, becomes easier to tolerate; hate and desperation are diluted with time.

I remember Jacoba and I sitting on a seat in the Kastanienallee last September; we could not talk, we just wept. And today one looks forward to a decent dinner! One lives in a sort of vacuum, the horror of present circumstances cowering somewhere in the subconscious. It was in September too that the terrible plan took root in the Hahn family to make an end of their lives. I had to watch how this idea grew, I had to witness the despair in Jacoba's usually clear eyes, and I fought with my entire being. When I was alone I had to picture to myself every detail of this ghastly possibility. Even during my darkest moments I could not fathom the extent of their forebodings. They were convinced that what had happened in Poland would be repeated here, that cohorts of enemy troops would sweep across the country, leaving only destruction and murder in their wake. They were determined to preserve Fritz* from such a fate. They would rather have seen him dead than torn from them and left in merciless, foreign hands. Up to a point I could understand this, but nonetheless Jacoba and I continued to fight an often silent, but bitter battle in those days.

A similar one I fought with our good friend Frau Schlensog, who swayed helplessly over an abyss. On her fortieth birthday, her husband was called up. For years he had been teaching music at a school, and now he had to guard Polish prisoners at Itzehoe. They have no children and she just cannot manage without him. And what sort of existence do she and many others lead? Rations for a

---

*Jacoba's son, born in 1934.

single person are pathetic; 60 grammes of semolina and oats, 125 gr. butter per week, 1 lb. meat and sausage per month. For this she has to queue for hours, and there is no one at home in her icy flat to make her a meal. She has to face the rest of the day in frozen silence. For weeks on end she had no fuel and used to come to us half starved and stiff with cold. We arranged that she should come to us every Tuesday and this, she said, kept her going. I tried to make it a special occasion, with good food, a cosy room and always something to take her mind off her misery. After supper we would join W. in his library. I would make a cup of tea, a kind gift from Walter Goldschmidt,* and W. would read aloud to us. We got through a lot of fine literature, long short stories such as *'Wunnigel'* by Raabe, *'Der Jahrmarkt'* by Tick, *'Die Hochzeit des Mönchs'* by C. F. Meyer, and many more. Her return home was horrible, not on account of air-raid warnings like now, which drive visitors home before 9 p.m., but because of her long trek out to Flottbeck during the black-out. She had to wait endlessly for the tram to take her to the main station. On foggy nights vehicles were almost invisible, two shaded red lights announcing the tram gliding through the darkness. The station would swallow her up like a black cavern, and she had to fumble her way down stone steps into an overfull train, lucky to find standing room. On arrival poor Frau Schlensog still had a twenty-minute walk, often through deep snow. We gave her a small stable lantern with a little red light burning brightly and comfortingly. Thus equipped, her feet in galoshes, her woolly cap drawn right over ears and forehead, she braved many a winter night and told us that often other lonely night-wanderers would join her, attracted by the homely glow of her lamp. She always said she loved the moon, for it made her solitary walk more companionable.

Rarely has our good moon assumed such wide importance as during this first war winter. Everything depended on its gentle light : going to the theatre, going out to dinner, visits to the cinema. Even on cloudy nights one could sense its presence; a brownish, diffused sort of duskiness lay over the streets, never noticed before when there were streetlamps. Nights of full moon and snow have come to mean for me a new source of peace and beauty.

*Brother-in-law of Mathilde Wolff-Mönckeberg's eldest daughter Jeltje (Jella).

Every time Frau Schlensog came to visit us, I tried to smuggle a small surprise into her attache case, which would give her pleasure when she got home. Many a time I tried to persuade her to spend the night with us, but she would not. She was always hoping that she might find her husband on her return, and even if he did not come, she felt his presence more intimately within her own four walls.

Personally I hardly ever went out at night during those winter months. I do not see very well when it is dark. To begin with we stuck black paper over all the windows and doors and it felt as if we were sitting in a large coffin. Since then it's become a little more human. We have got roller-blinds now, also in the kitchen and over the front door, and as soon as the beloved daylight appears and the black-out is over, they can be whisked up. Such were our Tuesday evenings during the winter of 1939-40.

12 January, 1941.

Now we have reached the middle of January already; January, the month I hate most. At the beginning of each year I feel a huge inner restlessness, a kind of pressure that urges me on to light and warmth. Is it possible that one can get used to war? This question tantalizes me and I am afraid of a positive reply. All that was unbearable at first, all that was impossible to fathom, has by now become somehow 'settled', and one lives from day to day in frightening apathy. And then suddenly everything explodes to the surface again. I think that *our* personal life is despicable. We still have our comforts and warmth, we have enough to eat, we occasionally have hot water, we do not exert ourselves apart from daily shopping expeditions and small household duties. W. sits in his armchair and reads novels. I spend ridiculous amounts of energy making menus, scrounging small extras. Then I am overcome and hate my lethargy, get cross and resort to senseless accusations. Nobody understands this. W. is hurt, and well he might be, thinks I am getting at him and does not realize that I am only angry with myself; that I am so down-hearted because I fail in my daily duties and would like to throw myself into something much more worthwhile. I find it so difficult to appreciate that to struggle on, to remain 'divinely sober in one's daily tasks' ['*der heilig-nüchterne Tageslauf*'], might be just as important as the fight of the foot soldier, the pilot, the U-boat sailor. 'They also serve, who only stand and wait.'

To complete the picture of our first war winter, 1939-40, I must mention the huge white expanse of the Alster, which was frozen hard for weeks on end. And there are many more things which have come back into my memory. Practically every day I walked across the frozen river to visit the Hahns and, despite icy winds, when the sun was out it was most invigorating. Strangely enough it reminded me of high mountains because of the piles of ice and snow and the strong sunlight. Fritz went quite mad in the snow, rolled around in the glittering white powder and said he thought the Alster was made of gold. Jacoba and I used to discuss food, of course. She did not quite trust my talents to find the cheapest and best, which is her forte. I do so hate to join an endless queue for a few cakes or chocolates. Women stand patiently for hours, half dead with cold, stamping from one frozen foot to the other, rubbing their hands, puffing and blowing, with the same hopeless resignation on their faces which I remember so well from the days of the First World War. 'We never have quite enough to eat,' I wrote in my diary at the time, but that was partly due to my lack of planning and to [the cook] Fräulein Resi's lack of imagination, but most of all because of the unexpectedly cold winter. Potato transports just did not get through, were stuck in the snow and whole lorryloads were scattered and perished in the frost. There were practically no other vegetables, the market was always empty and one wasted time achieving nothing in the way of shopping. My poor W. had to get used to milk puddings and porridge for his supper and he ate everything without complaint.

Just before and after Christmas the war in Finland was before our inner eye like a white and frozen ghost. Russia sent huge forces to subject the unhappy Finns, who fought back courageously, but had to give in because nobody came to their rescue. On silent skis, clad all in white, they stalked and skirmished the Russians, defended their country and sent thousands of invaders to perdition. Then came the desperate struggle between us and Great Britain over Narvik. The Western Front was quiet but for small skirmishes, but in the North we pressed on relentlessly. Suddenly we were in Denmark, 'to rescue that poor little country' we were told. Oh you poor proud free little Denmark with your kind King! What could the Danes do but surrender? Everyone always surrenders when Adolf Hitler wants it. Norway became Britain's ally; Sweden remained neutral. Our airmen fought magnificently in the battle of Narvik. They were completely isolated and cut off; their provisions came by air lifts; all this in dreadful weather conditions, ice and snow. Many of us were convinced that England would win this battle in order to prevent an attack from Norway on the British mainland. But this hope remained unfulfilled. One of Ruth's friends, Charlie Overweg, was killed in this battle.

So many mothers wait day in, day out, and every night as well for news. I do so feel for them, for I can never free myself from restless worry about your brother Jan.* I thought of him every night when I walked home from Jacoba's along the Harvestehuderweg, trying to out-distance the rapidly increasing darkness, on my right the Alster sleeping under a white blanket, shimmering in the frosty dusk, pink then gently green with a silver crescent moon swimming slowly into the sky. Then I felt like one of the big trees, their branches truncated, their wounds exposed and sore in the cutting winter air.

On 20 January we had 24 degrees of frost and no fuel supplies got through. It was so strange to watch people's features in the streets set in an almost characteristic frozen lifelessness. My only joy during that winter were the letters from [Matthijs in] Chicago and [Ruth in] Wales which arrived after long intervals. I heard regularly from [Jella in] Copenhagen, and up till Christmas was even able to telephone occasionally. Suddenly on Christmas Eve I was told to my immense sadness that telephonic communication with countries abroad was no longer possible. Until 1 January I had also been able to send telegrams to Chicago, twenty-five words for eleven marks! I had to get a permit from the Chamber of Trade at the Stock Exchange, go with that to the Main Post Office and send the wire. I had a reply by return of post. But just when little Arnold [Matthijs and Hermione Jolles' eldest son] was born, they stopped me and I could hardly suppress my tears imploring the officials to give their permission. So Thys and Hermione had to wait a long time for my congratulations. The two babies were expected round about Christmas, one in Wales and one in Chicago, and I was terribly excited. Every time the doorbell rang I thought

*Mathilde Wolff-Mönckeberg's eldest son, who was in South America.

1   Tilli and André Jolles on their engagement, 1900.

2 The first page of Mathilde Wolff-Mönckeberg's manuscript.

it must be a telegram. Actually I heard about Rhys John's [Evans] arrival when I was having tea with the Embdens. W. phoned the message through : 'Ruth and son flourishing.' I was beside myself, because it came slightly earlier than expected and I wept big tears of joy into my tea. We received the same message three times, once from Jella in Copenhagen, once from Walter [Jella's brother-in-law] in Brussels, and once from Thys in Chicago. So in the end we became quite overwrought and hysterical when the postman shouted 'A telegram', and I couldn't open it, expecting subsequent bad news. I was so thankful when on 9 January the safe arrival of Arnold was announced as well and good news followed in due course.

Ever since the outbreak of war I have been visiting the two Embden sisters regularly once a fortnight. They live in a tiny flat at the Brahmskamp. How they live is a mystery to me. Their brother, Professor Embden, emigrated with his wife to Brazil, thank goodness. He left his two elderly and ailing sisters behind with a heavy heart. For many years we had no contact but now I am happy that our paths have crossed again and that perhaps I can make their existence just a trifle less difficult. They are two wonderful people. I have never heard them complain; they are not bitter. Our afternoons together are quiet and peaceful and are a source of relaxation for me. Tea is served daintily and there is always a little something to make it a special occasion. Perhaps you cannot imagine what life is like for Jews. Their ration cards are printed on the outside with a large red J, so that everybody knows at once that they are non-Aryan. All women have to add the name Sarah to their first names, the men Israel. They never get special rations, such as coffee, tea or chocolate, nor do they receive clothing coupons. After 7.30 at night they are not allowed out into the street; their radios and telephones have been removed. Practically every shop and restaurant has a notice saying 'Jews are not wanted here.' It is so vile and mean that I can only blush with embarrassment while I write this. But you and your children must know of this, that things like this are possible in Germany under our present régime. You will hardly credit all this, or the fact that we others have stood by and said nothing. And there are much, much worse things. Many people have committed suicide because they could not bear this indignity. Then, like vultures and hyenas, they [the Nazis] rush in and grab the belongings of the dead; honest names are smeared with filth, and decent Germans have been driven to emigrate by the thousand.

The endless winter of 1939-40 was over at last, after weeks and months of darkness and icy frosts, and never before did we bless to quite the same degree every ray of sunshine and every tiny green bud. W. brought a daily bulletin about the progress of flowers in the park. Mimi* had been ill for many weeks, seriously ill. We put her in Ruth's room and were very anxious about her. There seemed to be only a tiny flickering flame of life in her emaciated little body. Spring was like balsam to her too. Thank goodness we managed to keep her out of hospital. In any case the hospitals are now almost exclusively for the wounded and victims of the 'flu epidemic. So she had to make do with my scanty nursing experience, was pathetically grateful and called me 'Sister Mathilde'. In a strange way it was a wonderful time for me. At long last I was able to repay some of her incredible devotion to you children. Sometimes she hardly seemed to be with us, lying back against her pillows with her eyes closed. I am sure it was her inherent strength and her desire to see you all again that kept that small flame going. Jacoba and Hahn had almost given up hope. One of them came every day, gave her injections and drugs, and even Hahn did not shirk the long journey, although he was very busy and had enough to do with the widespread influenza epidemic. I am not by nature a willing or gifted nurse, and many of the things I had to do for her went against the grain, but I was proud when she praised the compresses I made for her. Since Fräulein Resi had given in her notice for 1 April, we spring-cleaned the flat from top to bottom with the help of Frau Dostalski. W. did not go to Munich over Easter. There was hardly enough time between the terms. And summer came at last. I seemed to live only for your letters, for news from you and your children. The last letter from Ruth arrived via Antwerp, sent by the faithful Walter Goldschmidt, on 2 May. Then even that bridge collapsed and since there has been no more direct contact with my Ruth. On 23 April we received a Christmas card from Mr Reynolds [Hermione's father], sent on 13 December. We were still wrapped in a curious kind of vacuum, it was as if everyone was holding his breath, waiting for a new catastrophe.

I read in my diary that during April we went to a performance

*Marie Kleinmagd, Mathilde Wolff-Mönckeberg's faithful companion and nanny.

of *Figaro*; that every evening we read aloud to each other in English; that we tried to get used to our new home-help, Maria, with her curly grey hair, who used to bring extras, delicious items of food from her sister in Pinneberg, including eggs, five dozen once – and that I wrote and sorted out endless letters, cleaned all my drawers and visited Jacoba and Fritzchen regularly. We had gorgeous parcels from Denmark and from Thys through the Fortra Commission. At the beginning of May the atmosphere became extremely tense and very worrying with terrifying forecasts about England in the newspapers, and personal anxiety about Jella and Hellmuth. Yet everybody here was full of confidence and noisy triumph.

On 10 May came the devastating news : Germany had invaded Holland and Belgium! I happened to be down at the corner shop. Screams broke out on all sides : 'Have you heard the latest, have you heard the latest?' The radio went mad with special announcements, and nothing but loud martial music in between. All flags were ordered to be flown for ten whole days! Nazi flags wherever one looked, red like blood, a sea of blood! Despair – complete separation from Ruth, poor Walter handed over to the Nazis by the Belgians and French and carted off to a concentration camp in the Pyrénées. That afternoon we went to tea with [her brother] Franz and [his wife] Irms. Franz, proud of his captain's uniform, spoke only of victory, while Lulu [her sister Louise Sieveking] and I were completely desolate and shattered about our children abroad and about our poor Germany. Half an hour later Franz had his marching orders. Now there is no more contact with Ruth – for how long? How ghastly is a family gathering like that! The clinking of teacups, gay voices, happy anticipation on the one side, deep deep depression on the other, like being swept out to sea on a murderous tidal wave. What a Whitsun! News came from all sides of victorious infiltrations; the bombing of Rotterdam and Antwerp; the vain but desperate resistance of the Dutch. The abdication of the King of the Belgians; Queen Wilhelmina's escape to England. And the British are bombing Freiburg! twenty-four dead!* Jella writes

---

*There is still controversy about who was responsible for the bombing of Freiburg im Breisgau on 10 May, 1940, the first mass bombing attack of the war. However, in 1956 the Institute for Contemporary History in Munich reported that the raid was the result of a navigation error by a squadron of German bombers.

that for the fourth time in their lives there is a chance of a job in Buenos Aires. I write to Ruth via Chicago. We act like automatons – you cannot imagine what it was like to be in the midst of fluttering red flags and people screaming of victory. Behind us, in the background, there is only the grim picture of fight and extinction.

W. had bought tickets for a performance of *Wiener Blut* for Whit Monday, he thought it might cheer us up. We took Jacoba and Edith [Mönckeberg, her sister-in-law]. Edith is desperate too. She has heard nothing from [her daughter] Sybille in Australia, only knows that her husband is interned, if not a prisoner. [Edith's son] Jürgen's business in the Argentine is at a standstill; and [Edith's daughter] Renate's husband can't sell any more pictures because the Americans and British have left Florence. Eva, the youngest, has had a baby boy, but her husband was called up as soon as war started. Roland [Edith's son] is part of the conquering army in France! However, the opera was gay and cheerful. No chance of a taxi home, because most of them have been commandeered and you have to pay a heavy fine if you are caught using one. Although we are in May, it is still horribly cold, and two pairs of stockings and woolly underpants have almost been grafted onto one's body. Again and again, accompanied by military music, we have special bulletins about our victories in the west. We do seem to advance amazingly quickly, and the French are just running away from us. The famous Maginot Line was penetrated from the word go. And what price are we paying? Which of those dear to us who joined up is still alive? Jasper [a nephew] is there, a second lieutenant.

On 15 May Holland capitulated. Now for England! We hear the 'England Song' everywhere. Our parachutists accomplish the impossible and are feared by all our enemies. On 17 May after supper I rushed to see Aunt Susi [Susanne Semler, her eldest sister], who was ill, and took her a few small goodies. On the way there I was accompanied by a bright red sunset; on the way home it was the big yellow moon. I felt terribly restless and full of foreboding, and true enough at 12.30 we had an air-raid alarm which lasted until 2.30. One whole road in Harburg was destroyed. The noise was fantastic, the sky was lit up by a huge fireworks display of exploding rockets of all colours. W. and I stood for a long time just by the entrance of the air-raid shelter, a thing we would not do now after more than 200 raids !* But I shall never forget that night, the boom of the anti-aircraft guns, both big and small, stationed in the Stadtpark, and the crashing of bombs. Our air-raid shelter was still very primitive. The older and frailer inhabitants of the block of flats took refuge inside; the young grouped themselves nearer the entrance and imparted their wisdom and opinions. After the all-clear, I made a cup of tea and then crept into bed with a hot-water bottle, worn out and deathly tired. How many similar nights have we lived through since then !

In a way it was at this point that a new chapter of the war started. Brussels capitulates and the very next night we have another alarm. It is very odd to be torn from one's deepest sleep as through the open window comes the dreadful hollow howling of the siren, a ghastly sound promising death. One jumps out of bed, pulls on garments with trembling fingers, stuffs a few precious things into a small suitcase, takes a blanket and pillow and dashes for the lift. It is the same in all the flats, doors are banged and people shout to each other. To begin with, during the first summer of the war, we were still very disorganized. Now we have strict rules : there are air-raid wardens, two fire officers, two messengers and a detailed duty rota. I am still disorientated because I have not yet been assigned any specific duty. If, during those summer months, I went quickly out onto the balcony, I was so fascinated and en-raptured by the fantastic display in the night sky that I almost forgot the devastating cause of it. In the middle of the star-spangled firmament, shining and glittering with myriads of stars, huge searchlights would send their sharp golden arrows, ten or twelve at a time, crossing and re-crossing, backwards and forwards, vying with the brilliant stars. Then a suspicious humming sound of engines, growing, coming nearer and the anti-aircraft guns would break into a terrifying scream to meet the enemy. The hunter and the hunted are up there in that beautifully decorated heaven, and those cruelly searching fingers of light remorselessly pick out and pounce on a small black dot, trying to tear it down, regardless of how many mothers, wives, brides, sisters and children will weep.

I could not bear the laughter and chatter downstairs in the shelter. I am sure they are all *very* nice people, but they could not or would not realize that death was in our midst. Once I actually

*'Raids' is probably an error for 'air-raid warnings'.

thought I saw him : a tall, thin, middle-aged man came down the cellar steps, wrapped in a wide cloak, his hat pulled down over his eyes. He sat quietly in a corner, while shrapnel was raining down in the street and the air was alive with anti-aircraft fire. Suddenly it was still. 'There'll be an all-clear soon,' somebody said. With that the apparition jumped up, his hat fell off his head and a polished death mask was staring at me. There was a deafening explosion, a frantic noise of broken glass upstairs, a red streak of lightning. A bomb had hit the house next door. There was a vast crater at the corner of the Dorotheenstrasse and Langenkamp, all the corner houses had their fronts ripped off, there was not a single unbroken window in the immediate neighbourhood and the wardens in the road were decapitated.

During that first air-raid we lost 29 dead and 53 wounded. Harburg had the worst of it.

After this we had to stay in the cellar night after night, every occasion being noted down in my diary. By 3 August, when we went to Munich, we had had 50 [alarms], now over 200. After eight or ten nights of interrupted sleep in a row we would be almost worn out, particularly those who had to go to work the next day; children and frail old people also suffered disproportionately. Schools closed before the holidays proper, and a new law was brought in, saying that after a night of alarms children should not come to school until 10 o'clock. By now one will not find anybody in school after a night of heavy bombing, and since late autumn most teachers and school-children have been evacuated to safer districts. Altogether many many people have left.

To begin with we had a most inadequate shelter, a long strip of cellar, where we sat side by side on uncomfortable chairs, shivering and yawning and being forced to listen to stupid gossip by footling peroxided women. W. and I often stood in the open door to the cellar, and sometimes I even perched on one of the high metal dustbins – things now strictly prohibited. Now two large cellar areas have been converted into a proper shelter. Everyone has his or her own deck chair, and the city authorities have even provided bunk beds. We have small wall lights so one can read, old carpets underfoot, cushions and even a card table for the gentlemen to play Skat. Very recently we have been issued with anti-gas equipment. A tunnel has been bored through all the basements right to the Dorotheenstrasse. One only has to kick through the thin partition, or use a hatchet. During the summer of 1940 we still had several children in our block of flats and I donated our old cot so that one or other little mite could lie down and sleep. This forced nightly community of thirty to thirty-five people was not conducive to happy spirits and I have found it quite awful at times. Hahn too used to carry the sleeping Fritz down into their air-raid shelter, where a bed was ready for him. On top of everything, no one ever talked about anything but the war, often only silly rumours. I hated it.

On 21 May Jacoba arrived in great excitement with the just-received news that our troops had reached the Normandy coast and were cutting off the enemy retreat by encirclement. The Belgian government had moved to Le Havre.

Jella wrote that the Buenos Aires plan was gaining more certainty. I'm torn in two. At last I receive a letter from Hermione with the news that all is well with them. But where is Walter Goldschmidt? If only I can somehow keep the threads of communication intact, that is my sole desire.

The progress of our troops is fantastic, they are driving a wedge right into the massive army of French, British and Belgian soldiers.

Then there are small daily mishaps and annoyances on top of or underneath the world disasters. I lose my beloved fountain-pen; I drop my spectacles on the kitchen floor at Lulu's and both lenses are broken. My left eye is full of inflammation and I have to see the specialist, Professor Hansen, who says I'm run down and need to rest. How can I rest? Thank goodness my fountain-pen reappears miraculously, having hidden itself in the lining of my handbag. It is like being reunited with a faithful old friend. Jacoba gave me a complete medical check-up, tested my reflexes and told me bluntly that my blood-pressure was too high. And just when I decide to rest under the sun-shade on the balcony, in comes Frau Burlefinger to say that the whole of Belgium has now capitulated. More flags, more excitement, more martial music! The cinema newsreels tell us the latest developments, and they are breathtaking. The devil has it all his own way.

Fritzchen has a gas-mask and looks awful in it. In order to get used to it, he wears it when he rides his tricycle. The only really nice thing is our reading aloud of *Münchhausen*; Trollope's thick novels also give us great pleasure.

The most hateful and beastly thing was my being fined for inadequate black-out curtains in my bedroom. The high little window opposite my bed was supposed to have shown bright light, according to two witnesses from the Sierichstrasse. A fat policeman came three times, inspected everything, fingered the material of the curtains and would not believe me when I said I could not sleep unless they were tightly drawn, since the window is just opposite my bed. No good, I was guilty, two people had seen me, and I had to pay a twenty-mark fine, was called a black-out-law-breaker. Full of fury I sent for old Wittig, the decorator, and got him to stick black cardboard over the window. That policeman advised me to be on the look-out for other miscreants and to report them! I have since noticed many inadequately blacked-out windows, but wouldn't dream of telling tales about other people. Denunciation is a horrible business and far too much of it is going on. Even in school the teachers are trying to find out from the children whether their parents are politically reliable!

Meanwhile the huge battle in Flanders continues and the British are trying to save themselves from being driven into the sea. They are escaping in small boats or even by swimming, but are ruthlessly bombarded. How terrible! One of Dunkirk's forts is ours. In the evenings we can again sit on the balcony and I wave into the sunset hoping that Ruth will feel my thoughts and that at that very moment she too is thinking of me. 'The spirit of God is not at a point far above us, it is right in our midst, in every brave deed, in every aspect of beauty can it be felt,' says Isolde Kurz. Again and again I discover quotations and verses by poets which give me great comfort. 'The creative power' which Charles Morgan talks about means so much; I can imagine it but do not possess it. The thought sweeps me off my feet, when Morgan talks about it, and it is as if I am suddenly able to perceive immeasurable light and clarity through a tiny chink in a door, such brilliance as obliterates all narrow pettiness and gives strength and succour.

19 May, 1941.

I really wanted to describe to you all the people we share the house with; their strange differences of character, their sometimes grotesque sense of humour, but I lack the courage at the moment, and the right gaiety of approach. Who knows how funny they think we are, the garrulous Professor and his stuck-up, silent wife. Quite a lot of people seem to have enjoyed our nightly gatherings, so much that they positively missed our group meetings during the winter months and arranged a party without an air-raid alarm on the first Sunday in Advent in our shelter, lit by candles, decorated with fir-tree branches and Christmas angels, serving hot toddy and biscuits for everybody. What an extraordinary world! And if one stops to recall the horror of the first air-raid in May 1940 when 29 casualties were counted with intense dismay, and compares it with the number of dead on 10 May, 1941, well over 200, then one can only despair about one's hopeless passivity in the face of such terrible occurrences.

Our town looks ghastly. At the Rathausmarkt, Stefansplatz, near St Peter's Church and the Mönckebergstrasse, alongside the main station, down by the harbour, hardly a window is intact; huge craters everywhere, rubble, burnt-out attics, destroyed property. Whole families have lost their lives. Bombs come howling through the air and explode with a wailing sound.

Today is the 19th of May and it is still so cold and wintry that one could imagine anger in heaven and disgust with our hopeless little planet. There is hardly any green, any blossom, only here and there a timid crocus or daffodil in a front garden. But my W., pathetically pleased with each newly unfurled leaf, stands and looks at it admiringly. We lead a very quiet life together, but I don't think he has any idea about how desperate I am at times. Ever since – months ago – I read a book about Stalin, his policy and the way he ruthlessly persecutes all political deviants, I have given up all hope of ever seeing your brother Jan again. I just know that until recently there *was* hope and now it is gone. My love for him, deep down inside me, has perhaps been covered and hidden at times by my worry about all of you. But it is always there at the root of my being, and when the news comes and he is gone for ever, then part of me will also die, although the agony of death will be prolonged. Was he persecuted, was he hunted like an animal, was he tortured and shot? I can see him : wide open shirt without a collar; I see his eyes, a contemptuous smile on his lips; I see him collapse. Maybe he said my name. But I must not give in to sentimental fancies, for truth is not fanciful. And perhaps it is *all* untrue. I am tortured by these endless questions, night and day. Should he ever return when I am dead, then he must read this, must know how much I loved him. He has suffered so many injustices ever since he was a little boy and perhaps he thinks, What good was all your maternal love which did not shield me from harsh experiences, which did not guide me along an easier path when I was young? I am aware of my failings, I can see my mistakes and now there is nothing I can do about it. Forgive me, my son.

[*Date unknown.*]

Whitsun is over, and after our icy cold May we have the first days of summer. With unbelievable speed the earth is decked with green, once again we look down upon a roof of leaves, not black dead branches, and suddenly there is colour too. Shades of light and dark lilac, coral-coloured redthorn, the gentle bells of golden laburnum, white balls of guelder roses and splendid varieties of rhododendron, compete in all imaginable hues. It is like magic, but it cannot spirit away our depression, cannot evoke the rightful gratitude for all these gifts of nature. A bright moon lights our night sky, and so far anxious predictions of new disasters have remained unfulfilled. All is quiet. This stillness has an eerie effect, nobody knows what is going to happen and one shrinks inside oneself in anticipation. The flat too is very quiet and one is more aware of the absence of disturbance during these long light nights. One wanders restlessly from one room to the next, looks down on the empty street, up to the pink evening clouds and imagines that the house is trembling. The unreality of this suspense is as cruel as the fiendish occurrences in the world. And yet – as in peacetime – little pleasure boats go up and down the river and explode into music and laughter, but with a difference.

9 July, 1941.

Today is the sixtieth birthday of my brother Adolf and I am thinking of him. I can still picture our last meeting in 1914, he in his field-grey uniform, upright and handsome, the grey soldier's cap on his beautiful head. He had been stationed in Güterbock for training since September 1914. Vilma [his wife] and I came over from Wannsee and had lunch with him and his many soldier friends. Then he took us back to our train, stood outside on the platform and waved to us for a long time when the train pulled out of the station. I leaned out of the window, watched him grow fainter and more distant, and knew for certain that I should never see him again. When we were children I suffered acutely from his quiet and unruffled temperament. I resented it and almost hated him. We lost touch as we grew up, and then he suddenly appeared in Freiburg im Breisgau – where we were living – as a student, somewhat down-at-heel, and from then on a very deep friendship developed between us. I would like to describe him to you. Outsiders saw him as an exceptionally good-looking, friendly, but slightly condescending sort of person, who bestowed his social graces royally like benevolent gifts on the lesser endowed. The very way he carried his head, the very knowledge how much to give and how much to withhold, left all but a few in doubt of his intrinsic generosity, gaiety and warmth. His reserve was almost impenetrable and only on very rare occasions would he allow a brief glance into his innermost sanctum, but at those moments one realized the unexpected width of his possessions. The soul of discretion, he would guard his own and other people's secrets without ever giving a hint of his knowledge, even when it concerned his nearest and dearest. He was very gifted, but he did not shine like my brother Carl, who would carry all before him with his charm. Adolf always preserved his dignity, and this smiling dignity was his predominant characteristic. In his heyday, when Carl entered a room, exuberant youth came with him, buoyancy, cheerfulness and vibrant life. Adolf lacked this quality. He was a little pedantic at times, the wise and shrewd gentleman, could contribute much to learned discussions, but would correct what failed to please his impeccable taste. He was never wrong, never made a mistake in any relationship. He was singleminded. Where he gave his love, he gave it for good. Not many were lucky enough to receive it, but he gave his affection to me and your father without reserve, and had he lived he would undoubtedly have been your best friend.

16 December, 1941.

It is hard to imagine that it is December again, that once more this impenetrable darkness covers the world, the *whole* world, and life is even more quiet, much more quiet than last year. Oh my children, I am very lonely. For the past four weeks my beloved W. has been very ill, and he is now in the Barmbeck Hospital under Professor Reye. At first we all thought it was a bad type of influenza – Hahn thought so too – with shivering attacks and a high temperature. His scalp was aching and he had aches and pains all over. After a brief drop the fever shot up again with exruciating spasms of pain in his back and knees and his urine test was so doubtful that Hahn advised us urgently to get him admitted to hospital for a second opinion. We had not had an air-raid alarm for some time, but the night of 30 November brought an attack of unprecedented severity, the worst Hamburg has had so far. Thank goodness W.'s temperature was down that day, but he was in bed of course, when at 8.30 the siren started to howl. I dressed him as warmly and carefully as I could and put him on the settee in the hall. Mimi went into the shelter. It was relatively quiet at first, but the distant grumbling and rumbling came nearer and nearer and then it was as if the sky had split open with noise and I was frightened to death right beneath that huge glass roof. What was I to do? In every letter Thys had begged me not to take any risks. We both might easily have gone down with the house, buried beneath the rubble. Doors were creaking, windows banging – I just could not stand it. I wrapped poor W. in blankets and we went down in the lift. I made him a bed on a deck-chair with rugs and pillows, and there we remained for three whole hours, while the world seemed to perish under the onslaught of bombs. If you had seen the good old Mittelweg the following morning, you would have understood my fear. From the Raabenstrasse right up to the Church of St Johannis not a window remained intact. Piles of glass-splinters and heaps of rubble, the house next to the corner one no more than a mountain of smoking ashes, a mother with three children buried underneath. Altogether sixty dead and many hurt and wounded. High explosives fell along the Alster leaving huge craters in the front gardens, several metres deep, and a comfortless winter sky was looking through the big gaps in the walls of houses. What a terrible sight! The husband of the poor woman who was buried with her children under the ruins of her house was in Berlin, expecting his family the very next day. They had stayed behind to celebrate the first Sunday in Advent with the grandmother. He returned to find everything gone, and himself helped to dig out the remains.

Most fortunately W. was none the worse for this experience, even seemed to rally a bit the next day. But on the Wednesday he again became very ill. On Monday, 8 December, at 9 o'clock in the morning the ambulance men came and carried him gently down all the stairs on a stretcher. We drove through the damp and dark morning to the hospital. I felt very strange, but everything was done quickly and efficiently and soon he was in a white bed in a white hospital ward and watched me unpacking his belongings. He was exhausted and in pain, and I waited with him until the doctor came. Professor Reye gave him a thorough examination and said he would report to Hahn. The nursing staff is excellent.

This was ten days ago. I go and see him every morning, making my way via Sierichstrasse, Barmbeck, Rübenkamp, traipsing up-stairs and downstairs from train to train, and then through the allotments to the big entrance hall of the hospital, where I have to show my special visitor's permit. I'm never happy until I open the door to his room and see him, even if his condition has not im-proved, his face as pale and sunken, his lips as blue, his recognition of me as faint as before. Yet once he can focus on me, he smiles a vague little welcome. Yesterday evening I telephoned Professor Reye to ask his opinion about W.'s state of health. When he told me how serious it all is, everything went dark around me. Jacoba too has warned me that I might have to live without my W.; and then when I looked at him, his hollow cheeks, his unhealthy pallor and his sunken eyes, I felt as if he had already crossed that threshold. My afternoons are long and still and lonely, and the letter box is always empty. No more post from the U.S.A.! That speaks volumes.

29 January, 1942.
My darling children, why are you so far away? Thank God I can give you better news. Your stepfather is on his way to recovery, is progressing a little day by day. He looked positively rejuvenated this morning in his pale grey pyjamas which I was able to scrounge for him – 45 coupons and 25 marks – and a haircut, which removed the straggly grey-white locks from around his ears and temples. Everybody was delighted, and Professor Reye came a second time just to say he had noticed the elegant splendour of hair and pyjamas! Sister Erna told me that W. is the focal point of serenity in her ward, he is a great favourite and people are fascin-ated by him and try to converse with him.

Many weeks have passed since I last wrote to you. W. has been away for seven weeks and I have had to compose myself in patience and forbearance. The verse by Goethe which Thys sent me at the end of last November has sustained me greatly. *'Drum tu' wie ich und schaue froh verständig dem Augenblick ins Auge, kein Verschieben!'* And of course there were moments of brightness amongst the many dark ones. Right until the middle of January it remained doubtful whether W. would get across that horrible mountain. His temperature was high, 39 degrees, his appetite poor, his general lassitude worrying. On 9 January I had a telephone call from Professor Hansen, in Lübeck, who had visited W. as a friend, not as a medical adviser. He told me in his quiet and reassuring way that, while at the end of December he had been very doubtful about the outcome of the illness, he now felt that W. was over the worst. This note of hope was so unexpected that tears poured down my face at the phone. It had been so hard to give the same hopeless news to all the kind friends who phoned me evening after evening asking how he was. I can hardly remember now what ghastly things went through my mind during that time. We have grown so close during these war years that without his warmth and ever-shielding love I would have sunk into everlasting loneliness and frozen cold. Fate has indeed been kind to me. Now with renewed hope, hope of unspeakable beauty, I continue my daily pilgrimages to the hospital. He *will* come back to me, will sit once again in his big armchair, reading and smoking. Now I can even bear the separation from you more easily.

It has been a cold and dark and cruel January. I have always hated this month, even when I was a child, and this one was particularly hostile. Snow and ice and biting winds, and daily more tragic news of young widows, despairing mothers, sisters and fiancées, with no end in sight for this misery. Quite apart from the horrors of war, from the thought of all the trials and tribulations which our troops are suffering in frozen Russia or burning Africa, the small daily anxieties have become a constant struggle, a fight for food, a fight for fuel, a fight for clothing and shoes. Everything is difficult, there is no easy way round. Not once, but twenty times you have to phone the laundry to have things collected, and then it takes weeks to come back. No repairs are done, spare parts are unobtainable, broken items cannot be replaced, everything is shabby. Many people are resorting to barter and exchange as in World War I, and offer half a pound of butter, a quarter pound of coffee, or a pound of sugar and six eggs for a pair of stockings or a piece of soap. Some still seem to have game and sausages despite shortages, others don't. The general aspect of the population is one of downtrodden shabbiness, mended stockings, threadbare coats, shoes down at heel. But the majority puts up with it all; they are cold and hungry, they creep into their damp dark shelters when the bombs crash down, and sacrifice their loved ones all over the world without so much as a grumble. I wonder if you are thinking of me at this very minute? I can see you all, I can feel your love, and I am homesick for you.

7 February, 1942.
Yesterday I read a lot of old letters from the Rosenhagenstrasse, the Gellertstrasse, and steeped myself in the past.* In a book by Tieck I read that people are inclined to live in the past or in the future, but rarely in the present, which is what one should do. I cannot imagine the future at the moment, do not dare to speculate and hope only that there will be a reunion with you all. For this reason alone I wish to remain well and strong, for this reason too I am afraid of old age. There cannot be very many more years for me. Each day ploughs another little furrow into my face, bends my back, blinds my eyes and thins my hair, and my thoughts grow weary. Today I am particularly tired and really should not write. I have just sent a greetings card to Frau Gertrud Woermann, who is celebrating her eightieth birthday tomorrow. Suddenly I remembered the days which I spent at the Woermann house in my youth, between the ages of thirteen and twenty-one. Adolf Woermann was a big shipowner in Hamburg, a truly 'royal' merchant, a man whose very posture expressed dignity and importance : a powerful personality. One day I must tell you more about him, also about the journey to London which his daughter Hedwig and I shared with him.

7 March, 1942.
This is the first Sunday not spent with W. in hospital. For weeks I've had a cold and since yesterday I've lost my voice completely,

---

*Before and for a short time after her second marriage Mathilde Wolff-Mönckeberg lived in a flat in the Rosenhagenstrasse in the Hamburg suburb Flottbeck. The family then moved to a house in the city, in the Gellertstrasse, and from there to Andreasstrasse 39.

so that Jacoba told me strictly over the phone that I was not to go out, for my own sake and for W.'s, who once before caught a cold which delayed his progress. Anyway, I could only sit stiffly and silently at his bedside. So here I am, drinking a solitary cup of 'coffee', eating a fresh roll with honey, ready to spend a long quiet Sunday writing and reading. Ruth dear, you wrote once in a letter to Thys, which was really meant for me and which I am copying out, that it is a necessary healing process to be alone occasionally to try to sort out one's thoughts. But today my coffee has failed to restore my equanimity and vitality; on the contrary. I am sad and pray to God for a tiny sign of life from you, just a word that you are alright. You too will know this desperate feeling of homesickness. How hard I find it to be patient!

There was a phone message from W. just now : why aren't I coming? Poor man, he too has to be alone this Sunday. Throughout the past thirteen weeks I have only missed visiting him twice, and often it was extremely uncomfortable to struggle through biting wind and whirling snow, over ice and slush. For weeks now they have said only another fortnight and he will be home. I am still hoping that the end of this month will bring his return. Then everything will be easier and brighter. The atmosphere here at home is not cheerful. Maria spends her days in grim discontent; Mimi is rapidly getting older and more narrow, she lacks the understanding needed for this time and age, but then how could she have it? When the news is at its worst she reacts with 'How funny', and breaks into a vague, senile little giggle. I find that hard to bear. Altogether my patience and forbearance with old people is rationed, although strictly speaking I am not very far off old age myself!

Once again I have worked my way conscientiously through the *Siebente Ring* by Stefan George, especially the cycle [of poems] called *'Zeitgedichte'*, and have tried to grasp and internalize their beauty. One is overcome by some of the fine and noble personalities he describes, compared with one's own smallness. I carry certain lines around with me constantly, they even sing on in my dreams, and I am sure that their influence is lasting, even if one does not realize it. I try to scale a ladder out of my iniquities, my failures, but often feel so hopelessly stuck. The time in which we live narrows rather than widens the spirit. The world in general tears at the elasticity of humans until the spring is totally gone. And there is no renewal. We are stretched to the utmost, but instead of a return to one's original shape and form, one remains taut and immovable, without buoyancy. That is how it strikes me at times.

Listen to what it says in today's Sunday paper. 'It is reported that in the south-east territory near the Ilmensee 100 German dive-bombers attacked troop concentrations. From dawn till dusk our planes showered bombs of all calibres onto Bolshevik troops. There was excellent visibility. Concentrated nests of anti-aircraft constellations were systematically destroyed by our courageous dive-bombers who thereby opened the way for the advancing army. In one place alone 250 tons of high explosives were dropped on the enemy. Eight hundred dead were left on the field of the German advance.' And one does not freeze in terror. One puts the paper aside without having taken in this horrible picture. Yet how can one rid oneself of this ghastly impression : heaps of mutilated and bloody corpses, amputated and torn bodies, some perhaps still alive, scattered across the earth? Surely this causes the dumb depression which is ever present. What is most terrifying is that one ceases to appreciate the size of such disasters, it is beyond comprehension. I am beginning to doubt whether the message in Goethe's poem, that one should look the moment in the eye with 'happiness and understanding', is still appropriate.

The big decisions of the year 1941, seen from our side, were that on 23 June we declared war on Russia, supposedly our 'friends', but suddenly 'those bloody dogs'; that the United States declared war on us on 16 December*; that Japan, our Axis ally, entered the war. During June and July huge masses of German soldiers rolled eastwards. At first they fought not only the Russians but also the extravagant heat of summer. Ceaselessly we advanced, leaving behind countless dead and wounded, men and horses, on the limitless steppes. Then, when an early winter set in, we had to call a halt. Weather conditions, the unbelievable cold and mountains of snow, combined with the violence of Russian counter-attacks, made further advances impossible. Doubtless you will know all this. But what you cannot know is how our German soldiers have suffered, their descriptions of hunger, frostbite, bugs, darkness and the vicious cold. This endurance test made every man into a hero. And for what – for what? So that we at home should not be

*The United States in fact declared war on Germany on 11 December, 1941.

sacrificed on the altar of Bolshevism! The newspapers are full of casualty lists. So many only sons, so many very very young ones, nineteen- or twenty-year-olds. All those mothers, hearts torn in two, do their duty silently in the daytime and at night sob without hope, without succour. Then there are those strange little yellow men, the Japanese, who spread like ants, quickly and slyly, across vast areas of land, conquering efficiently, despising death. Right across to India they have swept and crept. The treasure-house of the Dutch empire has collapsed and a Swedish newspaper announced: 'An Empire is sinking!' Where are the United States and England? Are they asleep? We sit in a tiny corner of this huge conflagration and have no idea what is in store for us, what our loved ones still have to endure.

Perhaps there are still moments of happiness for you with your children, as there are for me with Fritz. What could be better than a child with its unconscious certainty and joy. Bright-eyed, he comes in and tells me how they play at war in school, of the 'bloody battles' they fight, and how he volunteered to be a dive-bomber – although he isn't a bit bellicose really – and how he is building palisades at home and shoots from behind them, trying to hit his mother. The ammunition is empty loo-paper rolls. And then immediately afterwards he listens eagerly and sensitively to Elise Averdiek's peaceful old story about Karl and Marie, and thinks this gentle tale is lovely. But he draws only burning buildings, torpedoed boats and parachutists throwing incendiaries. He sees nothing sad in that, but he refuses to listen to the sad parts in *'Karl und Marie'*, when the little girl dies, that is too near to his world.

21 March, 1942.

Today I have very sad news for you, my beloved children. Ruth especially will be very hard hit by this. Your cousin Jasper was killed on 9 February at the Donesbogen in Russia. A grenade splinter penetrated the back of his skull and he died instantaneously. This was the wording of the announcement in the Hamburg newspaper: 'Jasper Mönckeberg, B.A.Chem., First Lieutenant of an Artillery Regt., decorated with the E.K.II, followed his father who was killed in the First World War, and died in the East on 9 Feb., 1942, aged 26.' It was signed by his nearest relations. I will copy for you his last letter which he wrote to his stepfather

[Wilhelm] Kollmar as a testimony of the unbearable suffering our soldiers endured during this most terrible of winters. Tante Vilma [his mother] gave me the news personally over the phone on the evening of 12 March. She knew, of course, how deeply we all loved him. In a letter to me he wrote that Ruth's photograph was always with him, that she was more than a cousin, a most beloved sister. It is desperately hard for his mother. She was justly proud of him and through him of his father, your Uncle Adolf.

This is Jasper's letter, dated 23.1.1942. 'Forty per cent of our men have got oozing eczema and boils all over their bodies, particularly on their legs, and for three months we have had to carry them along as best we can. You can imagine the heavy responsibility this entails for a regiment which is retreating and was constantly under heavy fire before Christmas and has been again since January 17! I need every man to service guns, look after horses, run messages, etc. Our duty periods stretch over 48 hours, with 2 to 3 hours sleep, often interrupted. Our lines are so weak, 20 to 35 men per company over 2 kilometres, that we would be completely overrun if we, the Artillery, did not stem the onslaught of the enemy, who are ten or twelve times stronger. The Russians have to advance about 3 to 4 kilometres before they attack. On January 19 they attacked with about 800 to 1200 men. They looked like a moving column of trees. At a distance of 9000 or 10000 metres I opened fire and was able to cause such disturbance that 60 to 70 per cent of them could not take up their right position. Some withdrew, some were killed. There was such a mêlée of targets that one could hardly shoot quickly enough and each company leader thought his was the most important target. I was behind my gun all day long and managed to hold the attack or at least cause diversions, so that after ten hours' battle they had only advanced a couple of hundred metres with 3 or 4 hundred men, and the Infantry had not fired a shot so far. The Infantry appreciated this and brought me hot coffee, rugs and fur boots. They relieved my totally exhausted telephonist every half hour and eventually carried me into the bunker, since I had been lying for $4\frac{1}{2}$ hours in the snow – 35 degrees of frost – could no longer feel hands or legs and was completely unable to stand. When I emerged again they had put straw mats and fur rugs on the snow for me. All through the night we could hear the slow creeping advance of the Russians, but could not see them because we were behind a ravine whose ruggedness made movement in-

visible. You can imagine that sleep was out of the question. I
thought that I would never ever thaw out again. At dawn the
enemy staged two lame attacks, but thanks to our heavy firing they
petered out, leaving many Russian dead. In the afternoon there
was a further attempt, much shooting and noise, and then they
started giving themselves up. They reported enormous losses, certain sectors having shrunk from 130 to 20, some from 80 to 13 men.
Unfortunately our neighbouring division suffered a Russian infiltra-
tion. The enemy gained 20 kilometres on January 20, a further 8
kilometres on the 21st, right at our back so that I had to turn my
guns north and north-westwards. On January 22 a Panzer division
came to our aid from the south and we managed to halt the Russian
advance. At this moment they are still behind us, but moving
northwards. They are beginning to shy away from our front, a good
sign that they have had enough for the moment. Thank heaven for
that. I've had enough too, but it was terrific. If it weren't for this
swinish cold! And yet in the end I suppose it helped the defence.'

Whit Monday, 25 May, 1942.
Two months have passed since I last wrote to you. The picture of
Jasper on his horse is now with me always and he lives on in my
thoughts. I am often in touch with his mother. My heart goes out
to her and I can imagine her desperate sense of loss. She spends a
lot of time in Jasper's room, amongst all his belongings and those of
his father. The thought that all this happened to her, that everything is 'In Memoriam', gives her no peace. Do you remember that
happy Whit Sunday, my Ruth, only four years ago, in 1938? I was
still convalescent from my long illness and Jasper came to stay with
us over the holidays. You were so light-hearted and 'full of beans',
like two young puppies, despite the fact that you, too, had been
through a miserable period. You went for a trip to the seaside with
Fritz Caspari and some other friends and returned sun-burnt and
giggling. You had been swimming, had taken photographs, had
picnicked, and you had taken your beloved accordion along. Have
you still got it? The last time I heard you play on it was in March
1939 in the lounge at Laura Place, Aberystwyth. You were singing
and dancing, you were wearing your lovely Rumanian blouse and a
long black silk skirt, and you swept us all off our feet, even the
stout Professor David E. whose eyes became quite misty with ad-

miration. There were some lovely photos of that Whitsun excursion, you rather scantily dressed, playing your 'music animal' as you called it. If I had them here, I would kiss them now. Those were good and happy Whitsun days. Jasper belonged to us, particularly to you, and you called him your old Japs.

This year Whitsun is very quiet, only we two 'old ones'. It is cold and grey despite the voluptuous profusion of flowers outside, never really warm. One cannot think of sitting outside. W. came home on 1 April. I fetched him and the leave-taking from the hospital was quite touching, with presents for all the staff, who were waving goodbye, even wiping away their tears. It was wonderful to have him home again. At first he still needed quite a lot of nursing, couldn't manage on his own and I was very happy to help him. Now he is almost his old self again, only everything is slower than before. He has massage for his leg every day and is making progress. Today we went for quite a long walk along the Bellevue and back through the Sierichstrasse. Twice a week he gives his lectures here in the flat and we have to clear out the room and use all available chairs. There are twenty students, eighteen girls and two men. He is thrilled to be able to work again and intellectually is as sprightly and lively as ever. Compared with him I feel stale. This winter, with its never-ending cold and darkness, has taken its toll of my energy, and only now do I realize fully how tiring the daily hospital visits were, how my whole being was reduced by worry and anxiety. Suddenly my feet have gone on strike, but thanks to special supports in my shoes, which I get through a prescription from Hahn, are better now. I love fast movement, quick walking, and dreaded the idea of limping slowness. I don't want to complain about myself, otherwise I would have to add that I am losing my hair, my eyes are getting worse, and my neck looks like that of a tough old hen, etc. Really there is nothing to worry about apart from the weaknesses of my character. I gave myself a really good once-over the other day, I'm ashamed to say during one of W.'s lectures. While he was talking about Marlowe, Greene and Shakespeare, I was besieged by all my negative qualities : impatience, intolerance, ingratitude, etc. I wonder if one day all the prefixes 'in' or 'im' can be omitted, and I shall be satisfied with my patience, tolerance and gratitude? There are even more negatives which I do not want to enumerate.

And the world? One prefers to close one's eyes and ears, to try to

forget the horrible confusion which becomes more and more
baffling. Nobody has a clue where it will lead us. One does not ask
any more, simply succumbs into lethargy, just keeping up with
daily chores and the difficulties of rationing. One grows ever more
sensitive to the emptiness inside and the greed for the unobtainable
becomes more intense. Glowing fantasies multiply in tantalizing
colours when one thinks of large juicy beefsteaks, new potatoes and
long asparagus with lumps of golden butter. It is all so degrading
and miserable, and there are people who call this a 'heroic' period.

During the night of 4 May our house was hit by an incendiary
bomb. Previously the unhappy towns of Lübeck and Rostock had
had devastating air-raids, and big areas were razed to the ground.
We had been told that Hamburg would be next on the list, that on
the centenary of the nineteenth-century fire of Hamburg the
torches for a new conflagration would be lit again. And, true
enough, the sirens started to shriek during the Sunday night, warning of disaster. It was W.'s first time in the shelter since his illness.
No sooner were we downstairs – he was lying on a deck-chair –
than the hellish noise started and everything began to shake. It
was as if somebody was emptying a large sack of heavy stones over
the house, rattling and crackling, and at the same moment there
was a blinding flash in the street directly in front of the house, and
I shouted : 'The whole of Andreasstrasse is going up in flames!' As
I spoke we heard the caretaker's whistle : 'Fire, fire !' Panic ! Young
Pinkernelle rushed into the cellar and screamed, 'Where's the key
to Professor Wolff's flat, it's burning in there !' I don't know how I
got upstairs. I was met by thick smoke belching from our hall, and
bright flames just next to the good old grandfather clock. We had
been hit by four incendiaries, two in Frau Burlefinger's flat, one in
Herr Senkpiel's, and one which had gone right through the Senk-
piels' kitchen into ours. The stink and smoke were suffocating, water
and sand everywhere, but within ten minutes the fire was quenched.
Opposite, across the canal, the entire top storey of a block of flats
was alight. Crackling sparks, smoke driven in belching puffs, and in
between long yellow and red strands of fire licking upwards on
gusts of wind. On the other side in the Andreasstrasse bright flames
shot out of a window and the corner house was just one big conflagration. A stick of bombs had made a direct hit. The raid didn't
stop until 5.30 a.m. and even then there was no peace.

14 June, 1942.

Oh my darling children, now I am a grandmother of two new babies, a small granddaughter Anna Evans born on 25 April and a little Jolles boy in Chicago, whose name and exact date of birth I don't even know. Six of my grandchildren I have never seen, isn't that terrible? Yesterday I had a message from E. A. Macsmith from Geneva about a new grandchild and I behaved quite childishly, sobbed and cried and made myself quite ill with longing. I love you and your children so desperately and I am hollowed out with longing, devastated by the fact that only my thoughts are with you, that I am empty-handed but for my desire to be with you. What do the little Anna and Arnold's tiny brother look like? I hope both young mothers had an easy time, with no complications, are well and happy and able to feed, and full of hope for the babies' futures. Nobody here knows what your thoughts and feelings are, and you will probably be equally worried about us. I wish I had some of your clear-headed and trusting serenity, my Thys, or are you also lost in doubt at times? Are you sad, and does the wish overcome you to shake and break the iron gate that separates us? We were told the other day that we must live only for this war. I cannot bear that idea and will not listen to it. I live only for a better future and occasionally feel the indescribable joy of anticipating a reunion with you.

We go on living in much the same way. Sometimes there are good, warm days, then it is cold and grey again, and the weather mirrors the common mood. It is not true what the newspapers reiterate, that the German people stand steadfastly behind the Führer. Trouble is brewing in our midst, women groan, men curse, and everybody knows that yet another winter of deprivation with even less to eat is quite unbearable, that it might lead to a huge catastrophe. And yet we are oh so patient! My apothecary, staring into the rain the other day, mumbled to himself, 'The weather is mad, the world is mad.' And this echoes the general opinion. I have already been to the furrier to have my good old fur coat repaired for next winter and was told I could not have it back until Christmas as the only work they do is for soldiers for next winter in Russia. Seven weeks ago we had that incendiary bomb and the fire damage in our flat still hasn't been repaired, it looks just as chaotic. The old grandfather clock has been fetched, but it too won't be ready until Christmas. It is the same with everything, there is nothing to be had in the shops, no envelopes, no paper serviettes, no shoe-laces, no boot polish; you rush around and find nothing, return home exhausted and disheartened, and if you are lucky you might have got two envelopes or ten cigars. For the first time since last November, W. ventured into town last week. He even went by tram, wanting to attend a lecture at the University. All was well and he returned with Hahn and Professor Hecke, who each brought their little parcel of sandwiches. I made a small pot of tea and they tucked in to their meagre rations. No one is able to entertain any more. Bread, butter, milk, meat, flour, everything is closely rationed and only once a week do we get vegetables on coupons. We have eaten asparagus just once this year, half a pound per person. There is nothing to use for preserving. Last year we still had baskets full of beans, peas and broad beans and masses of eggs. My watching those three men eating their sandwiches was a typical war picture. I had had my bowl of porridge with Mimi and Fritz beforehand. Yes, Fritz has been with us this past fortnight. Jacoba unfortunately is in hospital, suffering from a duodenal ulcer, and once again I have my daily pilgrimage along well-worn paths, this time with Fritz for company, but now through colourful allotments, at least the last part of the way. She is much better already, has put on three pounds, special food and the quiet rest have done her good. I was very worried about her. She has done far too much recently, caring for young Pressentien, which exhausted her body and soul. She visited him every day for eight weeks during his final illness, did her utmost to alleviate his suffering towards the end with loving gentleness and medical knowledge. He waited for her impatiently every day and finally she went at night as well. He did not want to die, but had to. What a dreadful fate for him and his parents, who only last year lost his brother, also through T.B. and diabetes. What some parents have to go through!

Sunday, 19 July, 1942.

Again I have to give you tragic news, my far-away children. Your brother Jan is dead. I received a thick letter from an unknown lady called Frielinghaus in Othmarschen, who enclosed two other letters, one in German correctly addressed to the Gellertstrasse [where she used to live], the other one in Spanish with a peculiar address. Both contained the same information : Jan is dead. He died on 5 April, 1942 in Quito, Ecuador, having suffered from a serious stomach and bowel infection, and having been operated on on 1 April, 1942. The two men who wrote to me speak of him with deep affection. The German, a certain Herr Gebel, aged fifty-four, writes with the love of a father. He shared lodgings with Jan during his final illness and Jan died in his presence. I shall copy this letter for you. For a long time I had somehow searched for this confirmation of my fears, and yet I realize how keenly and strongly the hope had remained to hold him in my arms once more. Suddenly all is empty and over, and I stare into this vacuum where, up until now, my thoughts encircled a living Jan. Even my tantalizing fears and worries were better than this silence.

The lady called on me the following day. She told me that since her divorce she had worked as a nurse in Ecuador, and when Jan heard that she came from Hamburg, he asked her to come and see him. She met him only a few times, but when he was in hospital they had a long and lively conversation. He was delighted when she brought him books, and he wanted to know all about Hamburg, said she was to give me his love and tell me that he hoped to come to Europe next year. He was at the very hub of things, a respected and treasured member of his circle. As ever his life had been full of curious adventures. He had owned a cinema, worked in a pub. He did not speak about his wife and sons. But there was a little note, which he wrote to his friend Gebel prior to his operation, asking that his wife be notified of his death. Somehow he must have expected it. The lady said that in the big hospital ward amongst many sick people, he was conspicuous because of his rosy cheeks and his big dark eyes. He still spoke German fluently. It appears that there is quite a large National Socialist party over there, whose leader is a particularly unpleasant man who discredits every German who lives there. This leader courted Jan, probably because he judged him rightly to be a person of some calibre. There are diaries and the beginning of a novel, both I'm afraid in Spanish, which will be sent to me. Of course I am waiting impatiently. I might yet find some explanations. I assume that he never wrote because he had changed his name and could not let me know. But he thought of us.

This is Herr Gebel's letter. '11 April, 1942. Dear Madam, I have asked Frau Annemarie Frielinghaus, *née* Hansing, to hand you this

letter. Most unfortunately it contains tragic news. Your beloved son
Jan Jolles, known to us as Manuel Cazon, died in my presence on
Easter Sunday, 5 April, at 7 o'clock in the evening at the hospital
of Eugenio Espejo. He underwent operations for duodenal ulcer on
31 March and 3 April, both performed by doctors whom he knew
and with whom he was friendly, but alas the outcome was not
successful. Frau Frielinghaus and another gentleman from Hamburg, Herr Langpap, will be able to give you more details. In case
it might render you a little comfort, dear madam, I take the liberty
of telling you that your son was much, almost touchingly, loved by
all who knew him, on account of his modesty, his sense of justice
and his unselfish kindness. Personally I should like to say that he
was too good for this world. I tried to hold him back at times,
which he accepted gracefully, since I am that much older and more
experienced. I have just noticed, looking at the date, that it is my
54th birthday. I have before me a small scrap of paper, a quarter
the size of this sheet, which was handed to me by a young native
patient only a couple of minutes after the passing of my beloved
friend, written, it appears, on the day before Jan's operation. It
reads as follows : "Dear Herr Gebel, you know you are my last and
best friend, that goes without saying. Here are the keys of my suitcase, which I left at Pozo's house. Ask for it and keep the case as a
memento. Cash the enclosed cheque and give the money to our
comrades. Try and contact my wife, Antonia Banegas, Calle Peru
860, Santiago del Estero, Rep. Argentina. Yours, Jan Jolles." I
have shown this little note to Frau Frielinghaus and Herr Langpap.
I cannot send it to you, because a couple of creditors have appeared
and I need this proof to obtain the suitcase. But be assured, dear
madam, that everything is being done as your dear departed would
have liked it. We buried him on Monday, 6 April, at 11.30 in the
morning at the cemetery of San Diego. May he rest in peace! Frau
Frielinghaus has kindly agreed to convey to you the first few
chapters of a novel from his pen, called "Generación Perfida". He
wrote it during his stay of almost two months in hospital – as from
19 February – hoping that he would win a prize in a North
American competition. May I express, dear madam, the most heartfelt condolences and the salutations of a compatriot. Yours with
esteem and devotion, Georg Gebel.'

     Next I will give you the translation of the Spanish letter.

Letter from Polidoro Arellano Montalos, Quito, Ecuador, South America. 12.4.1942.

'With the deepest sorrow I fulfil the last wish of my beloved, too soon departed friend Jan Andries, and write to you. During the middle of February of this year Jan Andries contracted dysentery. On the 17th and 18th he had a very bad stomach ache but he did not think that this was a recurrence of the duodenal ulcer which he had suffered from before. This, he thought, had been cured during his stay in Germany. He was admitted to hospital on February 19 and after most careful tests, it was indeed diagnosed as a duodenal ulcer. From then on he had the best care from both the doctors and the nursing staff who prepared him for an inevitable operation. Everything was done with such concern that he was quite content. The operation took place on April 1 under good auspices. But it appears that his illness had spread, that ulcers had invaded his intestines, that there was more than one in his stomach. Despite most careful and intensive nursing, he developed intestinal paralysis. All efforts to combat this proved vain, and by 8 o'clock on April 5 we, his friends, were bereft for ever of his presence. He left us.

'Jan Andries is mourned by many people. He was honoured and loved by all who knew him, admired for his wide knowledge and his special gifts. He was one of us, we trusted him and he found peace in our midst. The circle of his friends was exceptional, he never had any difficulties in making contact, because his position in our society was favourable. He was a person of initiative, of charm, of fine education, all the prerequisites for attracting people into the orbit of his work. On April 6 we buried him in the cemetery here. His grave bears the name under which he was known to us, Manuel Cazon, and he rests in plot No. 1271, row 5. A couple of days later, we, his friends, formed a group at the cemetery, bringing floral tributes and making speeches to honour his personality. Jan Andries' friend Herr Gebel will send you some unfinished, but important manuscripts. He died forecasting the triumph of his country. I deem it important to give you all these details because it might comfort you to know everything. Because I am one of those who mourn Jan Andries' death most profoundly, who admired him so greatly, I should like to think that he bequeathed a bond of friendship between me and his family. May I therefore express to you my most heartfelt and sincere sympathy for the loss of a son who loved you fondly. He was a "caballero", respected in all spheres of society, an educator of the young, and as far as I am concerned, I would like you to feel that you have a friend in Ecuador on whom you can always depend. Your friend and servant, Signed.'

26 July, 1942.
Jan, you were always one of my far-away children and now there is nothing left of you but a large far-away question mark. Why, why, during those long years did you not write just once to let me know that you were still alive and thinking of me? My thoughts are pushing me against your sick bed, I am telling you that I have always loved you, always thought of you, that you should not have left me without looking at me once more. You do not know how it hurts that you went without my being there.

On 4 September, 1941 I wrote in my diary :

> Where are you, son? Many a lonely night
> I watched and waited for you, could not sleep
> And called your name into the silent dark,
> Prepared in eagerness for your return.
> Imagining your footstep in the street,
> I opened wide the shutters and the door
> To welcome and embrace you, but alas,
> The echo gone, I was alone and cold.
> Into my bed I crept and in my dream
> I held you, grown-up child, against my breast.
> Year in, year out and during night and day
> I never, never ceased to think of you.

There was a huge air-raid on Hamburg during the night. Four incendiaries fell on our house, and there was fire everywhere! Our flat, particularly the entrance hall, looks ghastly, for the second time almost submerged under rivers of water, clouds of dust, smoke and thick black dirt. The very opposite of Schiller's words : 'Without admiration we look on while all our possessions are destroyed.'

Boxing Day, 26 December, 1942.
My darling children! Before we see the end of this year I must write to you all. Every evening, when the black winter sky covers us

like a mighty dome, I think of the small grave in San Domenico; of
Jella and Hellmuth, Leopold, Franziska, Ernst and Michael; of
Jacoba, Gustav Heinrich and Fritz; of Antonia, Julito and Ottito
and Jan's lonely grave; of Thys and Mynie, Arnold and Martin; of
Ruth and Ifor, Rhys and Anna* – and send my love into the silent
world, which is silent only in my imagination. In reality there is
nothing but noise, the screaming of a thousand guns and grenades,
the explosion of bombs and everywhere flames and death and
desolation. Can you think of a greater horror? If one could look
down from the sky onto the world, all one would see would be a
circle of fire right round the earth and not just hollowed-out craters
and flying rubble, but also sinking, burning ships, furious seas and
aeroplanes torn asunder in the air. In all the cities, wherever they
might be, right up in the icy north, in the hottest south, in snow-
covered Russia, everywhere weeping, deserted women, mothers,
sisters, fiancées, everywhere field hospitals full of mutilated young
bodies. Isn't that too awful to imagine? And it has been like that
right through the year, is likely to continue until everything has
been destroyed and youth has been exterminated. I wish I could
write of something cheerful, but I know of nothing.

Last year we thought we had never had a quieter Christmas.
This time it was even quieter, only W., Mimi and I, no tree, just a
beautiful big fir-tree branch with gilded fir-cones and a yellow
candle which shed its light on the pictures of Jan and Jasper. I
hope you had a happier and more festive time. With children
around it could hardly be otherwise. Today Jacoba and Hahn are
coming for tea, alas without Fritz who is poorly and who would
have cheered us all up. Through Jella and Hellmuth's kindness we
had plenty to eat, in fact we were so full last night that it felt like
the good old days and we could hardly eat any more. So you have
no need to worry. Last night I had a peculiar occupation – you will
laugh, as I did – cutting loo paper, while W. read aloud to me.
Tante Ida [Emil Wolff's sister] sent us a lot of small cookies, each
individually wrapped in tissue paper, and since we are so short of
this important commodity, I smoothed them all out carefully and
made them into two handsome bundles. And I remembered my
own little mother, who always did this most conscientiously, although she could have surrounded herself with thousands of toilet

*Her children, sons- and daughters-in-law, and grandchildren. See family
tree on pp. 22–23.

rolls. But no, she used to buy oranges in crates, each one wrapped in tissue paper, which she carefully straightened with her clever and quick little hands with incredible speed. There now, I have found something funny to tell you after all!

Since we came back from Munich [where they visited Ida Wolff] in October, I have spent my time translating Jan's manuscript, and that was the best thing I could do. I have forced myself to learn Spanish and managed fairly well. Now it is nearly finished and I wish there was much more. I was so near to him that sometimes I felt as if my dead son was actually standing in front of me, glad of the opportunity to have me all to himself, which he had so often craved for. I have no idea what will become of his memoirs. They are not without danger for you, and maybe it would be best if I took them with me into my grave.

2 March, 1943.

Yes 1943! The dreadful holocaust continues to sweep across our little earth, and wherever you are, you too will hear the crashing and thunder, will feel how slowly but surely all that is good and valuable is being destroyed. People here are curiously apathetic and dull. On their faces one can read despair, can sense wretchedness, irritation and exasperation wherever one happens to be : on the tram, in the post office, in the shops. How different the atmosphere is from that of the first war year, when at the slightest provocation red Nazi flags were flown, drums were beaten on the radio announcing victory, and everyone bragged outrageously. Since the capitulation of Stalingrad and the realization of total war, all is grey and still. Shop after shop has closed down, one tolerates discomforts, forgets that life was ever different. Even my pen is getting tired, guesses that it will never be repaired, that ink is getting scarce, that the impetus and will to write are waning. Behind the photographs of Jan and Jasper there is a vase of yellow tulips; sometimes there are proud white hyacinths, stiff like carved images of bells. I am so grateful that I can have flowers again. The bad-tempered little woman at the end of the street often lets me have a few extra because I cannot resist buying some almost every day. We also have to be grateful that the winter was so mild. There were only two days of severe frost, January 12 and 13. Apart from that it was mild, often sunny and quite warm. But out east it was bitter. Onkel

Franz reported 35 degrees of frost. He has been right in the thick of it, came home on leave briefly in November and told us of the frightful eeriness of partisan warfare. His last letter was about the necessity of withdrawal, hoping they would still make it. One can't believe a word of what the newspapers say. Months have passed by like this since our return from Bavaria in October, one day like the next, and with no hope of ever hearing from you. Only Jella's letters come every week, a tremendous comfort, and she always writes cheerfully, even if there are worries in the background. We know nothing about dear old Walter Goldschmidt, while Hellmuth's sister Elisabeth has made a daring escape and is safe. The details of this are incredible, like an exciting detective story. If the need arises, what can't one do?

We are told that Berlin had a terror raid last night. Last week it was poor Cologne's turn, and probably we will be next. We also had to go down to the shelter last night. No one beds down for sleep these days. We sit stiffly on hard chairs, ready to jump up at a moment's notice, and superficial conversation barely hides the inner tension. The gentlemen no longer play Skat. Every time we go down with bags and suitcases, I wonder if we will come up again and what our flat will look like. There have not been many alarms, but they are bound to come. It is warm in our flat and thanks to the bad-tempered, grey-haired pearl Maria, we always have decent meals. However, W. declares that he is never quite satisfied, that he finds it hard to concentrate on his work, and I have an insuperable longing for something sweet, to go to the sideboard and quickly pinch a spoonful of sugar or jam, although I know how scarce it is. Everybody, not only us, looks unhealthy and prematurely old. My neck looks like a disgusting old hen's gullet, I'm ashamed of it and cover it up. But what of it compared with the universal fear? The only thing that takes us out of ourselves is music, which we have revelled in this winter. Guided by W. and clutching his arm, I gladly braved the darkness which envelops you like thick black cloth after the performance and the ensuing struggle to get one's coat and hat. The worry about air-raids is always there, but something lingers on and gives comfort. The marvellous slow movements of Haydn, Beethoven, Brahms and Mozart make me want to dissolve. I would love to dissolve, but one remains hardfaced and bitter. Circumstances are not auspicious for better and softer thoughts, not for me anyway. I fight losing battles with my own iniquitous impatience, with the fact that almost everybody gets on my nerves, except Jacoba and Fritz, and try to comfort myself with the speculation that I may be undernourished, lack vitamins – but I'm afraid it is just my bad character. 'Please be nice,' you used to say, my Jan, and I do try, but. . . .

And what else happened this winter? Peaceful afternoons with Tante Lulu, reading Stifter, who has the same effect as music. Many almost happy hours with Fritz either in the Klopstockstrasse or here, and a never-varying rapport between Jacoba and me. My two sisters and I had subscription tickets for matinees and saw moderately good performances of plays, most of them rather third rate. But we, of course, the three sisters Mönckeberg, retained our 'dignified postures', occupying seats in the stalls. I had some nice lunches out of town at the Elbchaussé with my schoolfriend Lieschen Sieveking-Binder, *née* Dunker, in her cultured home with its big garden. We also met for cosy evenings with Heinz and Rösi Sieveking [her cousin and his wife] at the Zickzackweg, Rösi much reduced in size and Heinz as nice as ever. All are different milieux, about which I could write reams. Another time. Today I must write a note to Herbert Martin Weber who sent me a pound of dripping from Norway. He is very faithful and always remembers us. My most private life I spend at my desk with Jan, translating his memoirs. I have almost finished and feel sad. I also keep on learning poetry by heart, and by now I have a rich store in my head. Lines and whole verses go round inside me, often for days at a time. I have just been to the bathroom. I looked at the soap – a lovely piece of real soap still – lying at one end of the soap-rack, a dry sponge at the other, a big gap between them like an invisible wall. I was thinking of our separation and how far apart we are. How good it would be if the sponge would cease to be dry, would work up a good lather with soap and water and soak up the cleansing moisture! Goodbye my treasures, every one, big and small. Adio!

Böckel bei Bieren. 14 August, 1943.*
Four terror raids on Hamburg have all but destroyed the whole town. For weeks beforehand we had reconnaissance planes over night after night but *without* shooting. We always dressed very

*The Wolffs were staying with a friend, Hertha König, in Böckel bei Bieren, Westphalia.

3 Tilli Wolff-Mönckeberg (left) with Mimi, *c.* 1930.

4 Mimi and Ruth, *c.* 1930.

6 Emil Wolff, c. 1938.

5 Tilli in 1938.

quickly, but then sat in the library, suitcases packed and ready by the front door. We were told the British would avoid Hamburg because they would need the town and its harbour later on, and we lived in a fool's paradise. We listened with horror to the reports about the frightful raids on Cologne, Essen, Bochum, Dortmund, Duisburg, Wuppertal, of which very little is left. It was a pitiless destruction of everything, cathedrals – both Cologne and Aachen – factories and houses being blown sky-high, and human beings rushing into the river like living torches. Descriptions were so ghastly that one could hardly believe them. Yet we still thought we would be safe, even when leaflets were dropped : 'You have got a few weeks' respite, then it will be your turn. There is peace now, then it will be eternal peace.'

I remember the evening of 16 July when we went with several friends to the Curio Haus to have supper after an excellent lecture by Professor Bultmann. Afterwards we went home with the Snells by moonlight, discussing all eventualities. Frau Snell intended to take their two daughters to Bavaria and her husband was to follow. Little did he know that he would have to go as a homeless person, having lost everything in a fire. There had been similar evenings like this one throughout the season. Snell was in charge of the German-Greek Society and had engaged some first-class speakers, among them Professor Reinhard who spoke brilliantly about Thucydides. W. too gave a fine talk on Shakespeare and Antiquity, had a packed audience and most appreciative acclaim. Our little suppers afterwards were most popular despite surrender of food coupons. We nearly always had a satisfying and tasty fish dish, soup first, and a suspiciously multi-coloured jelly pudding. The men even scraped the sauce boats.

But before I return to those days and nights of horror, I must remind you of the fall [*sic*] of Stalingrad, a situation where everybody held their breath for days and weeks on end, particularly terrible for those who knew nothing of their relatives, still know nothing for that matter. After the surrender at Stalingrad Goebbels declared *total* war to all at home. Everyone was called up, even women up to fifty years old, and mere boys had to do anti-aircraft duties. Only old people like us were allowed to keep domestic help. Jacoba had to report for duty too, but was seconded for the time being because she was helping her husband in his practice. She was also allowed to keep Margot [her maid]. Then came the new excite-

C

ment over the battle of Tunis [April-May, 1943]. We came here
for ten days over Easter and were glued to the radio every night. It
was then that we heard of the first big victories of the Americans
and British, who advanced quickly, surrounded our troops and took
prisoners. That left the way open to Sicily. We hoped and hoped
that things would move even faster, rumours spreading like wildfire.
People seemed to have forgotten all the sick old jokes about our
high and mighty leaders, one knew too much by now and was
completely disgusted.

Since the spring, Hamburg has been covered with artificial fog
whenever there is an air-raid warning. The city disappeared below
a thick grey sauce, which, when Hamburg re-emerged, had dis-
coloured and shrivelled up leaves, hedges and grass.

My delight was unbelievable when, on 22 March, I received a
letter from Ruth, held in my hands a piece of paper covered with
her writing, in English, such a dear, dear letter. A little later Baron
Lagerfeld brought from Stockholm via Fru af Petersens a photograph of Ruth's children, Rhysi and Anna. I cannot tell you what
moments like these mean to me, how I still drink this draught of joy
and strength to the very dregs. Our Maria, whom we call 'the
moody', not 'the bloody', did some spring-cleaning and even a little
preserving. She is always bad-tempered, miserable and envious, but
she is very industrious. Once when I reproved her for her insolence
and reminded her how well off she is, she retorted, 'You'd better be
quiet, Frau Professor, otherwise I might spill one or two things
about you.' What a sweet character, so lovable! She is always sending poor dear old Mimi on messages and then is rude to her on top
of it. Fritzchen has been ill, alas, for quite a long time, had to miss
school and just never quite got rid of an ear infection. Then he
contracted scarlet fever and was really very poorly. I was allowed
to visit him, read to him for hours, nearly all the books by Karl
May and the whole of *Robert, der Schiffsjunge*. He called me his
reading machine. I also read aloud to my blind old friend Frau
Schneider, and we got through a lot of Eckermann on our Monday
afternoons till fate tore us apart. The summer was damp and cold
practically the whole time and we hardly ever sat on the balcony.
Then suddenly we had an extreme heatwave and simultaneously
came Hamburg's final destiny, exactly one year after I had the
message of Jan's death, and after my two dear friends Gertrud and
Käthe Embden committed suicide.

24 August, 1943.

Today little Ernst [Goldschmidt] is ten years old. How I wish that he will grow up to become a successful and happy human being; how I wish that he will fulfil all his promising gifts, and will become a credit and comfort to his parents, develop into a fine and rich adult in the truest sense of the word!

We have been here in Böckel for nearly a month, and it has not been an altogether smooth ride. The aftermath of those terrible days has frayed our nerves, and more than ever we battle against irritation. W. is incredibly prickly; no doubt through his former associations with this place he is extra sensitive, which makes him harsh and impatient with others. He can barely forgive Hahn now that he is 'cock of the roost' here, and resents the fact that Hertha is obviously more interested in the younger, rather than in the older friend. And really Hahn is in the midst of a deep depression, having no clue what the future holds for himself or his family. As far as the Medical Association in Hamburg is concerned he has extended his leave, but nonetheless he went back to Hamburg, also to Hanover, to try to reach some kind of conclusion. He makes plans only to reject them again, and is painfully restless. Jacoba really wants to return to Hamburg to help in any way she can, but that is impossible because of Fritz. Children are not allowed to return, and their flat has no window panes, only glass splinters and dirt, no water, gas, electricity or telephone, like every house in Hamburg. This eternal coming and going is not easy for us women to bear. First and foremost we feel only immense gratitude compared with others, and are prepared to shoulder small inconveniences, together with the incomprehensible demands which this kind of life imposes upon us. It is stupid to get so upset about the rules of this house, for instance, that one has to take one's shoes off before coming in, that our hostess does not like smoking indoors, that she wants to select with whom of her guests she would like to talk. We are treated to delicious and plentiful meals, beautifully served, we sleep through undisturbed nights in clean soft beds, and live in surroundings which exude peace and a serene atmosphere of summer. Every day we see colossal loads of hay trundling through the fields and listen to the sound of threshing. Flocks of sheep cover the meadows in grey woolly waves; black and white cattle lie, chewing the cud, against a background of green; and to Fritzchen's particular delight the fat sows, noisily lapping up their mush, roll about in the brown mud. I am enchanted by this district. Nothing but wide yellow cornfields, gently swaying in the wind, green meadows wherever one looks and on the horizon a distant chain of hills and a seam of forest; no official footpaths, no other farm buildings and in the wood complete stillness between berries and thorns. The house is unique with its moat and rugged turrets. Our rooms are in one of the turrets and are most comfortable. Every room in the house contains a rare collection of solid, well-kept furniture, carved and painted cupboards, big chests that inspire confidence, glass-fronted shelves with beautiful porcelain, pewter and brass, superb carpets and valuable paintings, and alive between all this, huge shining bowls of dark red roses. One could almost forget what brought us here : our poor burning destroyed Hamburg. Up till this moment we have been told of 100,000 dead,* but not nearly all have been found and counted, and one million inhabitants have left the city.

Now I will tell you exactly what happened. It was a perfect sunset on 24 July – the anniversary of Hendrik's death – and W. and I were sitting on our balcony, discussing what would have to be done if one of us were killed. I asked him particularly to continue being a friend and father figure for you all, and he wanted me to care for his sister Ida. Then we went to bed, hoping to have a good night's rest. Shortly before 1 a.m. the air-raid warning goes. As always we dress in a hurry. But before we even reach the shelter a veritable thunderstorm of noise explodes above us. It doesn't stop for even a second, one detonation following another without respite. The house shakes, the windows tremble and it is completely different from any of the other times. Everybody, including the ailing Frau Hafekin from the first floor, and the Leisers with their baby in its pram, races for the cellar. The light flickers and flickers, but doesn't go out yet. For two whole hours this ear-splitting terror goes on and all you can see is fire. No one speaks. Tense faces wait for the worst at every gargantuan explosion. Heads go down automatically whenever there is a crash and features are trapped in horror. My one thought is : God save Jacoba and Fritz, and make me ready to face the end. At last it gets quieter, the inferno recedes into the distance. Back in our flat we stand on the balcony and see

*An overestimate. Hans Rumpf in *The Bombing of Germany* (Müller, 1963) puts the number of deaths caused by the mass bombing of Hamburg between 24 July and 3 August, 1943, at 30,482.

nothing but a circle of flames around the Alster, fire everywhere in our neighbourhood. Thick clouds of smoke are hanging over the city, and smoke comes in through all the windows carrying large flakes of fluttering ash. And it is raining in torrents! We go into the road just for a moment at 3.30 a.m. In the Sierichstrasse several houses have collapsed and fire is still raging. The sight of the Belle-vue is dreadful, and the Mühlenkamp is nothing but glass and rubble. We go to bed completely shattered.

There is no proper daylight the following morning, the town is so shrouded in smoke. The sun cannot fight its way through, but looks like a bloodshot eye onto the devastation. It remains like that all through the day; the smell of burning is all pervading, so are the dust and the ash. And the siren never stops. Maria is in such a state that every time it sounds she makes a dash for the cellar with flying hair and apron strings, and we do not get anything to eat until 5 o'clock after another very heavy day raid, which was worse for the Hahns than for us. Jacoba told us about it afterwards. They cowered in the cellar, Fritz between them, holding a big cushion over his little blond head. The noise was so colossal, and everything shook and trembled so, that they made up their minds there and then : we must get away at once! She telephoned in the evening and told me of their decision; I still thought they were exaggerating and tried to calm her. The following night we had another alarm, but not such a bad one, and on Monday I decided to go and see the Hahns. To my surprise there were no trams and I had to trudge along in the boiling heat. The Harvestehuderweg looked grim, every second house burnt to the ground, gaping windowless holes instead of glass and frames, and, worse still, in the Badestrasse and Mittelweg huge blocks of flats had collapsed. Jacoba was in a bad state, Fritzchen as happy as a cricket. W. joined me there having been to the centre. He was full of sad tales. His beloved cigar shop no longer existed, his favourite luncheon place, Michelsen, des-troyed, huge devastation at the Gänsemarkt, a direct hit on the Opera, Eimsbüttel and Grindel wiped off the face of the earth. We huddled together, feeling very depressed. Suddenly Gustav Heinrich appeared, much excited, with another gentleman, a patient of his, who was prepared to evacuate Jacoba and Fritz within the hour to a place outside Hamburg, where he himself had found shelter with his family, having been bombed out for the second time. Jacoba had furious objections, did not want to be rushed, said she had

masses of things to prepare, Margot was not there, etc., etc. But
Hahn was firm, and they did indeed drive off soon after we left
them. They all went to Sprötze near Buchholz. We went home and
had another raid during the night, but only a short one. On Tuesday Hahn returned, went to his psychiatrist and got a recommendation for four weeks' sick leave. I visited my dear blind friend Frau
Schneider that afternoon in the Marienterrasse and found her in a
room where the door to the balcony plus frame had been torn out
by the blast. But she was quite calm as usual and, full of gratitude,
told me how kindly they had been treated in the air-raid shelter of
the small Pension Helbig next door. Just imagine the warden in
charge of all these old people, some lame, some blind like Frau
Schneider, helping them unhurriedly into a nearby shelter in the
middle of the night! And that under very heavy bombing. We sat
together peacefully and talked, although we could not concentrate
on reading, and decided to meet again soon, little knowing that the
very next night might tear us apart for ever.

During the night of Tuesday-Wednesday there was yet another
terror attack, such a heavy one that it seemed to me even more
horrifying than the one we had had on Saturday. After the siren
had gone, there was only a little shooting at first, then all was quiet
and we thought it was over. But then it started as if the whole
world would explode. The light went out immediately and we were
in darkness, then a tiny flickering light. We sat with wet towels over
nose and mouth and the noise from one direct hit after another was
such that the entire house shook and rattled, plaster spilling from
the walls and glass splintering from the windows. Frau Leiser
fainted and lay on the floor, her sweet baby was frozen with fear,
nobody uttered a sound, and families grabbed each other by the
hands and made for the exit. Never have I felt the nearness of
death so intensely, never was I so petrified with fear. With every
explosion we thought the house would come down on top of us,
that the end was there; we choked with the smell of burning, we
were blinded by sudden flashes of fire. And then stillness.

The following morning Maria reported that all women and
children had to be evacuated from the city within six hours. There
was no gas, no electricity, not a drop of water, neither the lift nor
the telephone was working. It is hard to imagine the panic and
chaos. Each one for himself, only one idea: flight. We too – W.
raced to the police station for our exit permits. There were endless

queues, but our permits were issued because we had a place to go to. But how could we travel? No trains could leave from Hamburg because all the stations had been gutted, and so Harburg was the nearest. There were no trams, no Underground, no rail-traffic to the suburbs. Most people loaded some belongings on carts, bicycles, prams, or carried things on their backs, and started on foot, just to get away, to escape. A long stream of human beings flooded along the Sierichstrasse, thousands were prepared to camp out, anything rather than stay in this catastrophic inferno in the city. During the night the suburbs of Hamm, Hammerbrock, Rothenburgsort and Barmbeck had been almost razed to the ground. People who had fled from collapsing bunkers and had got stuck in huge crowds in the streets, had burning phosphorus poured over them, rushed into the next air-raid shelter and were shot in order not to spread the flames. In the midst of the fire and the attempts to quench it, women had their babies in the streets. Parents and children were separated and torn apart in this frightful upheaval of surging humanity and never found each other again. It must have been indescribably gruesome. Everyone had just one thought : to get away. W. tried vainly for some kind of vehicle. Most people in our house made hasty impromptu arrangements, carrying bits and pieces into the cellar, and we also stowed away a few things. Since nobody could cook, communal kitchens were organized. But wherever people gathered together, more unrest ensued. People who were wearing party badges had them torn off their coats and there were screams of 'Let's get that murderer.' The police did nothing. We had another alarm during the night, but only a short one. Maria stayed the night with us because she had had such an awful time in the bunker with the heat and the stink, collapsing people, drunkenness and overt aggression, howling children everywhere.

On Thursday morning we still hadn't found a solution and were very near to despair on account of the general atmosphere of panic. Furthermore, it was impossible to wash. No sooner had we precariously lit a little fire in the big old kitchen range and fetched a jugful of water from the cellar, than the siren went again and everything had to be left as we raced into the shelter. Suddenly there was a knock on the door, the bell having ceased to function, and who was there? Jacoba – pale and trembling, but it was really her! We rushed into each other's arms and howled. 'You've got to

leave today,' she said. 'I will come and fetch you in two or three
hours in Herr Splett's car. He is a patient and will do it for you.
Get ready!' Oh you angel of salvation! Off she went to her own
flat to fetch lots of things and we hunted around like mad, packed
various things, stowed others away in the cellar. Maria disappeared
to her brother and from thence to her sister in Etz. By the afternoon
everything was neat and tidy, what edibles were left were handed
over to Frau Senkpiel and we had just a small suitcase each. I do
not know how the five of us stuffed ourselves into that tiny car. We
sat on our suitcases, legs tucked under, terribly squashed and hot.

Driving through the devastated town was so frightful that I shall
never forget it. The little car shuddered over mountains of debris,
we had to navigate around piles of rubble and stones, torn-out
waterpipes, blocks of concrete and in between the charred corpses
of human beings and horses, ghastly sights. And then suddenly we
were in open country, heather-covered fields, and we stopped in
Sprötze in front of the small railway post-house, where the Hahns
had found asylum. It was crowded and primitive, but oh so
good to be with helpful, sympathetic people who gave us all a good
plentiful evening meal and allowed us to camp down in the actual
post office. We were so exhausted that after a short walk we retired.
Streams of refugees came and brought reports that it had been
given out on the Moorweide during a food distribution that a vast
reprisal raid had been made on London, a thousand aircraft had
rained down bombs for hours on end. Totally untrue, of course!
No sooner had we drifted off to sleep than the siren started to
scream and we were witnesses to the fourth enormous terror raid
on Hamburg. We stood outside the front door for two hours
watching wave upon wave of heavy bombers droning their way
towards the unfortunate city, listening to the distant crashes of
continuous thunder, marvelling at the never-ceasing rockets of fire,
the falling of burning, shot-down aeroplanes in a night sky dotted
all over with millions of stars. What was left of Hamburg? We were
told the following day that all Winterhude was razed to the ground
and gave up all hope of ever seeing our home and our belongings
again.

We were all assembled for breakfast at 6 o'clock and at 7 the
train left for Böckel. The Hahns were ready to follow the next day
with all their things. At about 3 we poor refugees arrived with our
small suitcases, dusty, dishevelled and worn out, and were wel-

comed with open arms. What a strange feeling to arrive like this, unannounced and suppliant. No wonder it was so hard for W., as I have already told you. For me the worst was that I soon noticed how nervous Hertha was, how little she was really prepared for us. She had two friends staying with her, the painter Fräulein Sprenger and Fräulein Hübner, and was expecting further guests. When I confessed that the three Hahns were also on their way, her hospitality collapsed and she declared she just couldn't do it. I could visualize my poor Hahns and their despair but rushed to the phone to try to stop them coming. Fortunately there was no way of getting in touch with Buchholz for all telephone connections via Hamburg were cut off. (Only three weeks later we had telegrams from friends asking whether we were still alive, and postcards I wrote as soon as we arrived in Böckel did not reach Hamburg until a month afterwards. For weeks I knew nothing of my sisters and friends.) So I could not get hold of the Hahns, but sent them a long telegram, not knowing that this would not reach them either. I cried my eyes out and went into the kitchen where darling Mimi was busy stripping redcurrants. In the desolation and anguish of my soul, it was such a comfort to sit with her.

The following day, just before lunch, Hertha appeared in our room, pale and aghast : the three Hahns were at the station with all their luggage. I raced off through the midday heat and there they were, just as hot and dirty and weighed down as we were the day before. Hahn immediately declared he would never set foot in a house where he was not welcome, and I went back with Jacoba and Fritz. Hertha had meanwhile changed her mind, gave them a very warm welcome, sprang on her bicycle to fetch Hahn, in which she succeeded, and after this inauspicious start we had four glorious weeks; Jacoba had seven with Fritzchen.

Hahn travelled around constantly, went via Sprötze to Hamburg to have a look at what was left of our flats, and came back with the incredible news that both were intact, not even a broken window in ours, while everything around us was smashed. That Thursday night must have been particularly bad in our district. There were not many people left in our house, but those who were nearly perished through the density of smoke and the heat of the fires. Many had to remain in the bunkers until 11 o'clock in the morning, having been locked in because of the enormous fires. Hahn became more and more depressed and exasperated travelling around like that, and less able than ever to make up his mind. W. also went to Hamburg with Jacoba to fetch us some more warm clothes. Those were very odd days for him. Apart from the caretaker, Herr Senkpiel, he was the only living soul in the block of flats. He had to fetch water from the cellar and drank lemonade for breakfast. He only had a tiny stump of a candle and fumbled around in almost complete darkness, but he was very proud to have found all the things I wanted. He also brought me that desperately longed-for letter from Ruth, dated 29 May.

We decided not to go to Wiessee yet, but home first, because all empty flats might be commandeered. Again the journey was rather terrible. We missed the connection in Bünde and had to sit on our suitcases for an hour, and when we eventually arrived in Harburg – there were still no trains to Hamburg – we got into a terrifying crowd of people. The entry into our poor poor Hamburg I just cannot describe to you, a hopeless sight like that has to be seen to be believed. Rain was teeming down through the shattered roof of the Hauptbahnhof, and when we reached the Dammtor we were so exhausted by the heat, the heavy suitcases and the pushing and shoving of the crowds that we gulped down a glass of beer. And then finally only W. was able to get into the Underground with the biggest case and only as far as Kellinghusenstrasse. We two poor women, Mimi and I, had to walk home with the smaller luggage. We crept like snails along the Harvestehuderweg, resting every five paces, and after a painful hour eventually reached home. Then a climb to the fourth floor and upstairs a frightfully dirty flat with no water, gas or telephone awaited us. Only the electric light had been reconnected. It was not exactly a happy homecoming, you can be sure. But Mimi and I did not give in and started work at once. My room at the back of the flat was the worst, with a thick layer of ashes on the balcony. We had only left-over sandwiches from Böckel for supper.

The fortnight which followed was very uncomfortable and we realized how spoilt we had been. Lugging up water in heavy buckets from the cellar, dividing it carefully for use : for washing, for the evil-smelling loo, for cooking on a smoky range – all this was no fun. Yet how lucky we were to have our old-fashioned kitchen range. Things improved when Maria returned from Pinneberg. She brought us a boiling hen, but declared that she would not dream of having her meals at the little pub on the Mühlenkamp, where we had managed to eat quite happily every day at 12 o'clock while she was away. One very hot afternoon I managed to scrounge three cwt. of briquettes from a coal merchant, but we had to cart them home ourselves. Maria and I loaded them onto a small cart, she pulling while I pushed. Then they had to be stored in our cellar, but W. did that with a student who happened to be there. We could not get away to Wiessee, because our registered luggage from Böckel had not arrived. At last after ten days it came, and another kind pupil of W.'s fetched it for us on his bicycle. Now we could plan our journey, but I hardly felt like going any more. First we had to get Mimi off to Freiburg for a holiday with her relations. My poor W. had to walk with her to the station in almost complete darkness at 4 a.m., again heavily loaded and at Mimi's not exactly racing tempo. From there he took her to Altona, where she caught the train to Basle. We had a similar early-morning walk, quite terrible. Each of us was wearing three overcoats and I my fur stole as well, carrying two suitcases apiece. Frizzled, we reached the station in the dead of night, but the journey to Munich was quite comfortable. We had plenty of food, but nothing to drink, since there had not been room for a thermos flask. When we arrived the first thing Ida had to do was to give us gallons of apple juice. We had three good weeks in Wiessee and renewed our friendship with Frau Schlagentweit and the Rieppels, who took letters with them to send to Ruth and Thys. And in next to no time we were back in Hamburg, and once again had to face the impact of the destruction of that beautiful city. The journey back was not so good. We had taken our supper with us, but there were eight of us sitting in a second-class compartment. The lady next to me was smelly. She had with her a huge featherbed, which she had bought from a farmer, also an open basket which overflowed with woolly slippers, butter wrapped in newspaper, loaves of bread, fatty bits of sausage and none-too-clean underwear. We were due to arrive in Hamburg at 7 o'clock in the morning, but since Hanover had had a very heavy terror raid, we had to by-pass it and stayed outside Lehrte in open country for a long time, reaching Hamburg at midday, starved and tired. First of all a cold beer from a papier-mâché mug into our empty stomachs. Of course Maria had no meal for us and we had to make do with memories of kinder welcomes.

Jacoba came that same afternoon, was pale, tired, irritable and full of worries. Gustav Heinrich is not at all well, he is suffering from a severe depression, and our Fritzchen has been evacuated to the country, where he lives with completely strange, but obviously very kind people in Lindhorst, near Hanover, and goes to school there too. Jacoba has to take in a lodger, but first of all the window panes have to be replaced. Margot has come back. Every day there are longer and longer lists of casualties in the newspapers, of whole families, grandparents, parents and children, who have lost their lives during those catastrophic raids. Tante Lulu comes with a very worried expression, she has to leave her home and move in with us. All the old ladies who lived in her private old people's home for widows have been given notice. They have been given to understand that it would be best to leave Hamburg, better still to die! One can't do with the ancient. So I am trying to rearrange the flat, make it as comfortable as it should be and give it the extra touch of beauty with flowers. W. had only a cake for his birthday, a couple of letters and a visit from our only child, Jacoba. Both our laundry and our cobbler have been bombed out and I am trying to find substitutes. How hopeless everything is. The refuse-collectors hardly ever come and the streets are full of dirt and rubbish which bulges out of the dustbins. All this heightens even more the sad dilapidation of our street scenes. I have pushed my desk into the library near the window. The big settle now stands where the piano used to be, and the latter is in front of the sliding doors. It does not look too bad like that, and we use the hall for eating. The sideboard is out there, my small mahogany cupboard and Tante Lulu's mahogany table. It is a bit crowded with furniture, but there is still room to move. Only Mimi's room is full to the brim with bits and pieces. Meanwhile Frankfurt am Main has had a heavy terror raid. Tante Lulu moved in on 15 October. She is tired and disheartened. What a lot of moving around we have done in our lives. I am also helping Jacoba to rearrange her flat. She has got a little elderly couple, both hairdressers, to come and lodge with her. We shift furniture around, empty drawers and long for Jan and Thys who used to enjoy helping on these occasions. Tante Lulu's room really looks very cosy. I am fed up with queueing for ration cards. I join a long line of women and stand for three hours, crushed together, first on the road, then in danger of my life on a rickety staircase, finally on a landing, which becomes so crowded, and the women so offensive that I am pushed into a corner without the slightest chance of ever getting to the desk and the issuing clerk.

Darkness falls and I retreat home having achieved nothing. W. manages it the following day, but also has to stand for three hours in a mêlée of human bodies.

During this period we had a strange letter from Jella, signed by one Kläre Holm. It appears that Hellmuth is in Sweden. More worries. Soon afterwards comes the news of persecutions in Denmark and I am frantic with anxiety. Jacoba reported that many people had been ordered out of Copenhagen. And always more terror raids follow on yet more cities. Hanover is devastated. Poor Grandmother Hahn has lost everything, house and belongings, and has moved to Lindhorst to join Gustav Heinrich who has withdrawn into silent desperation. Then Berlin, enormous damage done, Leipzig and again Essen, Cologne and Kassel. We too are prepared for the worst, spend many hours in the cellar, night or day. We used to go to the nearest bunker at the first warning, but it was too awful, the heavy suitcases, the darkness and the shoving of wild people. Apart from that, we could not undress, had to sleep in our clothes, or rather not sleep, and certainly had no rest. Everyone is dead beat and completely exhausted. I often think of my poor blind friend Frau Schneider, who has lost everything and was evacuated to Lübeck to complete strangers. Her daughter Lanka was forced to close her business, has no idea what to do next.

We get very conflicting news from the Eastern Front, rumours most of them, but one thing is clear to all of us : a Russian breakthrough would mean disaster. 'Then there'll be nothing left but to take poison,' Frau Schlensog said to me quite calmly, as if she was suggesting pancakes for dinner tomorrow. The overall picture of this, our fifth war winter cannot be compared with any of the previous ones in its grim darkness. Added to the external destruction is that within us, which paints its furrows into every feature. We have lost courage and are filled only with a dumb kind of passive apathy. Practically everyone knows that all that bluff and rubbish printed in the newspapers and blazoned out on the wireless is hollow nonsense, and when big speeches are made nobody listens any more.

20 January, 1944.
Only today, long after the beginning of the New Year, do I get down to writing to you, my dearest, oh so unreachable children. I have been meaning to come to you, but ever since Christmas our

beloved old Mimi has been ill and I am fully occupied with nursing her. Once again it started with severe bronchitis and the higher her temperature the lower her spirits. We immediately got in touch with Professor Reye and asked whether he could admit her to the Barmbeck Hospital, but he said he could only accommodate her in the air-raid bunker. That would have been too depressing for her so we kept her here, not without very grave anxiety, for we cannot stay up here during alarms and it is impossible to take her with us to the shelter. However we risked it and heaven was kind, there were no heavy raids during the initial and most troublesome period. Christmas Eve was naturally very quiet. Maria went to her sister in Pinneberg, and we three, Tante Lulu, W. and I, sat round the small low table which was decorated with a fir-tree branch and four candles. W. read the birth of Christ from the Bible and we un-packed a truly voluminous parcel from Tante Ida. There was the gorgeous aroma of real coffee – everybody was issued with 50 grammes – and Maria's large cake tasted delicious. We ate and ate until we could eat no more.

My thoughts wandered back to many Christmases of the past, to the early ones in my parents' house, when all we nine children were still at home. What a display it was on the 24th! The large drawing-room was an ideal setting for this festive occasion; a huge Christmas tree stood between the windows, reaching from floor to ceiling, alight with coloured candles and covered with glitter, glass balls, chains, and delicious chocolate rings, little sausages made of marzipan or jelly, and the special Hamburg goodies called *'Benidt-kringel'*. We sat in the room next door and sang one carol after another, louder and louder in anticipation, and during the last verse of *'Oh Du fröhliche,'* when it says 'let all the lights shine', a little bell rang in the drawing-room, once, twice, three times, and the doors were thrown open. The youngest went first, the others followed. The feeling of blissful tension and expectation was in-describable. Anxious glances fluttered from one table of splendid gifts to the next, all round the walls of the room, wondering which would be one's very own; and when one saw something one had longed for – once it was a big birdcage with a green parrot for me – one almost choked with happiness and gratitude. And how many lovely and joyful Christmases I celebrated later on with you all! The first one after I was married was in our small palazzo in San Domenico near Florence. We started off by being enormously secretive about our purchases and then promptly told each other what we had bought. It was difficult to find a little tree, but our gardener Tonino managed to scrounge a real fir-tree in a pot. We decorated it in our accustomed fashion with all my Hamburg Christmas-tree decorations and its lights shone so brightly on the 24th that our *contadini*, the peasant caretakers and their children, gathered outside and pressed their faces against the windows of our conservatory to see the splendour. Your father and I followed tradition and sang all the old carols; I played the piano and had also practised a Handel aria from the *Messiah* : 'And he shall lead his flock'. When I came to the words, 'and gently guides her that is with child', we both wept a little. Then we had a sumptuous meal *à deux,* which was heavenly but did not agree with me! I'm afraid I was sick on my plate and my husband had to get rid of everything outside the front door, so that our maid Adelia should not notice anything. What children we were! And how different it was only two years later when our early dream of happiness was already shattered. By then we had moved to Freiburg im Breisgau, an attractive little university town, where your father had enrolled as a student. He, who had so far accepted no ties, was determined to do some hard and concentrated work and finished his doctorate in three years. While he was attending lectures and seminars, I sat in our house, which was far too big for a sad childless couple, waiting with devouring restlessness for my second child. Our little palazzo on the hill of San Domenico with its wide view across the Mugnone Valley over to the hills opposite and San Miniato, with the city of Florence and its Duomo down below, with its surrounding cypresses and flower-beds, with the *podere* and the Rinaldis cultivating the land around; our palazzo blessed with the gracious conservatory, spacious rooms, where the old Dutch and Italian furniture looked so alive and right on the stone mosaic floors, and our collection of brass ornaments glittered against the white walls; our palazzo with its vast kitchen, where a cauldron was always simmering over an open wood fire, and the kitchen itself never really looked neat and tidy, because everywhere there were too many nooks and crannies with strange insects and creepy-crawlies; where there was only one loo with an icy marble seat and most unhygienic; our lovely palazzo was nothing but a dream now, the only reality the small grave in the cemetery in San Domenico – a cruel reality for my whole life.

What a contrast was our new home, a normal bourgeois house in a friendly road, no garden worth talking about compared with Italy's luxurious profusion of flowers, numerous but quite un-romantic rooms, but completely lacking those nooks and crannies which no broom ever penetrated to disturb the long-haired cater-pillars, and with a proper lavatory and bath, where water was plentiful. Our odd assortment of furniture looked a little forlorn and out of place, and we ourselves did not really fit in as yet. At least that is what Mimi confessed to me later. She came to us then aged forty, which I considered quite antediluvian. She thought we were a lost little couple. The first Christmas in Freiburg was lonely, with no child's voice. Thank heaven the following year we had Jella lying in her blue basket-cradle under the Christmas tree; the year after that it was just before darling Jacoba was born, and soon Jan completed my trio. Oh my children, what better than to lose oneself in the past? It conjures up so many lovely pictures and I can hardly keep up with my pen.

But I must talk about this, the fifth winter of the war. Only sad, horrid visions pass before my inner eye, grey and dull, like a bad film-show. Nothing but heaps of rubble wherever one looks, hollow ruins of houses, empty windows, lonely chimney stacks, charred remnants of furniture, high up on a bit of wall a bath-tub, a forlorn bed-frame, a radiator or even a picture clinging precariously to the bombed-out shell of what was once someone's home. In this dismal weather it is a devastating scene. In the streets mountains of rub-bish are piling up. The big metal dustbins are never emptied and garbage is bursting out all over the place. Paper, potato-peel, cabbage leaves, the muck-containers open their lids like gaping throats, vomiting out their evil contents. Then the wind takes it all and scatters it over the wet roads, leaving a stale, foul stench. We are told that every street must dig its own rubbish pit to avoid further contamination. And this in our super modern and clean Hamburg! But it isn't our Hamburg any longer. Grandfather Mönckeberg would never recognize it. We are told that it will be rebuilt 'more splendid than ever'. On goes the film-show. Dark shadowy creatures creep towards the mountains of left-overs and stir them up with greedy hands, looking for something to salvage, something to eat. They are Italians in long brown coats, their caps still somewhat coquettishly perched on their dark hair. They are supposed to clear away the mess in hand-carts, but first they try to find something to still their hunger, chewing ancient potato and apple peel. They are members of the 'Badoglio Clique', so one is told, lazy devils who shun work, that is why they are ravenous. One is not allowed to speak to them, but I feel sorry for them. The other day I gave one of them bread coupons for 500 grammes and he touched his cap at least twenty times.

There are children everywhere, hordes of them. There is no school and they roam the streets all day long. Like the foreigners they forage in the garbage, dig tunnels in the rubble and imitate the siren to perfection. Women, their tired faces half-hidden in head shawls, climb over the debris. They have official permits to collect what is still usable. They cart away what they can, to build new homes somewhere outside town. Thousands sleep in the bunkers every night, not having a roof over their heads. It is amazing how these poor human beings manage to create something, some kind of homestead, out of the rawest of materials, charred wooden boards and broken bricks. Everybody lends a hand : the husband if he is at home, the wife and all the children. And they are so proud of their achievement, preferring to live like Robinson Crusoe in one single room on the lonely heath, rather than be billeted out amongst strangers.

Here is another instalment for my film. Two elderly ladies are dragging an enormous bundle of clothes to a laundry far out in the suburb of Stellingen. Nothing can be fetched these days for there are no vehicles, and there is no hot water to wash at home. Their journey is very cumbersome. Twice they have to change trams, have to wait endlessly and when one comes there is hardly room for them in the crowd. They have to stand on the platform with their heavy luggage. Icy feet and drenched clothes. But it is gorgeously warm in the laundry, where they find lots of bustle and friendly people. Quickly they dispatch their dirty bundles and receive the clean laundry. On the way home they are silently occupied with toe gymnastics to get their circulation going. Just as they reach the Dammtor Station, the siren starts its howling, warning song. They had been dreading this, and now everybody is pushing, stumbling and squeezing through the narrow entrance into the large bunker on the Moorweide. It takes some time to get in, the guns have started and aeroplanes can be heard humming overhead. At last our two ladies are inside with their bundles, are elbowed right up to the very top against their wishes, abused and scolded because of their awkward packages. All they can do is sit on their bundles, knee to knee with strangers and tired out. The atmosphere is sticky and appalling. Suddenly there is a thunderous explosion, once, twice, three times, and bombs crash down just outside the bunker, tear open the ground and leave wide craters. The bunker trembles like a drunkard, but it stands. Women scream and pretend to faint; children howl. That is an everyday picture. The two elderly ladies are Tante Lulu and I.

27 January, 1944.

You cannot imagine how incredibly full it is in our flat. Tante Lulu, as I have told you before, has our dining-room. In Ruth's former room – her spirit still inhabits it – we put Mimi and Maria. But when Mimi became ill, grumpy Maria could not tolerate that close proximity, and really I cannot blame her. Despite frequent airing, the room was stiflingly hot and we had to hang up wet towels for Mimi. Our poor invalid was also extremely noisy at night. When her horrid cough did not worry her, she used to moan and cry, 'Alarm, alarm,' then again she would snore like a wild animal. Sleeping next door, she often kept me awake for hours, poor darling. Where was Maria to go? At first our kind neighbour allowed her to bed down in her flat, but when her sons returned that was impossible and we really had a problem on our hands. In the end we put her bed in the entrance hall under the mirror by the telephone. I must confess that this solution was awful. Maria went to bed at 10 o'clock sharp and demanded quiet! So Tante Lulu and I had to withdraw at 10 and tiptoe past Maria's bed to the bathroom. One of us invariably bumped into her, or sent one of her slippers flying along the long dark corridor, which resulted in a furious growl from her. In the mornings we had to have our breakfast within sight of her unmade and tousled bed; the telephone could not be reached except by sitting on her bed. All these small irritations needed a lot of extra humour and fortitude, both rare commodities these days.

25 March, 1944.

Months of silence again! Many a time I wanted to come to you, but stupid little important and unimportant things prevented me. I fully realize that, compared with others, I am very lucky, spoilt even, and yet I cannot appreciate Maria's innumerable good points, cannot make the most of her undoubted qualities. Since our dear old little Mimi has gone away, I have a good deal more to do. She used to clean my own room so beautifully, brushed W.'s suits, darned his socks and underwear, polished the brass and silver. But surely all these jobs should not overwhelm me, as they undoubtedly do at present? I cannot get the right kind of rhythm into my daily tasks, feel tired and listless, and Jacoba says my blood pressure is too high again. Sometimes I wonder whether it is ordained that I have an early and sudden end? Everything combines to depress me : the view of the grey, crumbling ruins opposite and all around us; the wet, nasty, dull winter without frost and sun; the accumulated dirt which I have mentioned, and last but not least saying goodbye to my nearest and dearest. For weeks I dreaded the thought of Mimi having to go, it oppressed me like a threatening black cloud and we postponed the parting again and again. Yet the day came when Jacoba and I packed her belongings, while she looked on helplessly, tears overflowing her dear, faithful eyes. The next morning at 4.30 a.m. I took her to the station. We left the house in complete darkness, felt our way down the outside steps, fumbled like two blind people along the Dorotheenstrasse, not knowing where we had got to, and miraculously found the tram stop. We clung to a few other people who were also waiting. Jacoba had gone to Altona and fought for a corner seat. We pushed Mimi bodily into the overcrowded train, past a woman from the Ukraine who had just given birth to a child. And there she sat, my companion for over forty-one years, a tiny shrunken old person, and all I could do was to kiss her and wish her Godspeed before the train rolled out of the station. Jacoba and I sobbed all the way to the Klopstockstrasse and she said, 'One after the other is torn from us.'

Since then the flat has seemed deserted. All the time I imagine her dear old face with its innumerable creases and wrinkles, and I shiver; her love and her trust were so warm. God, how we used to quarrel at times, I often fought a terrible battle with my irritation, was intolerant and unkind. Some of her little habits drove me beyond endurance and I lost my temper. We had furious clashes, flung abuse at each other. She threatened to leave, and I to throw her out. A hundred times I accused her of being ungrateful, we started a slanging match, screamed at each other. She would run to her room, and I would follow her, scolding, until the tension

reached boiling point – and then suddenly we would laugh and cry
and fall on each other's neck. Right to the last moment this would
happen, but love and humour always won in the end. Relationships
like this are unique in life and when they cease, a lonely, icy gap is
left. What my life will be like without Jacoba, heaven only knows.
Yes, she is still here, and although we sometimes do not see each
other for days on end, we know the other is around, and we can
have long telephone conversations in the evenings. All this must
sound as if I am altogether lost and forlorn, and in fact I am so
lucky with my W.'s, your stepfather's, tender and warm care around
me. But my relationship with you children and with Mimi is so
totally different, belongs to the very depths of my innermost being.
Flesh of my flesh, blood of my blood, the intensity of this bond
between us, the shared interest in even the smallest things that
concern us, transcends all, can probably only exist between a mother
and her children. Through five years of war Jacoba and I have
shared an ever-increasing burden of suffering, and now we can
no longer carry this alone. The whole past winter was so incredibly difficult for her, that all one can say, of and to her, is :
'*Du hieltest, Du bist ringsum so bewährt, dass Dich was andere
brechen muss, nicht bricht.*' ['Your steadfastness has carried you
along, and what breaks others, cannot throw you down.' (Stefan
George).]

The Hahns have now decided reluctantly to leave Hamburg and
to move to Friedrichsroda, where Gustav Heinrich has been offered
a post running a clinic under a Medical Officer, Sanitätsrat Bieling.
To arrive at this decision was a long and difficult process, fraught
with obstacles, and they still do not really know whether this is the
best and wisest thing to do. But then who knows anything these
days? Nobody can make plans, nobody knows what is in store for
us, the future is more inscrutable than ever. There is something
almost absurd about our daily lives. You get up, the warning sound
of the siren in your ears, you make a plan to do this and that, but
then the whining howl starts again and everything comes to a stop.
A loudspeaker voice warns, 'Danger, danger, two bomber squadrons
have passed the city defences. Get ready, prepare yourselves!
Women and children into the air-raid shelters. Fill buckets with
water, have your sandbags handy, I shall be with you again in four
minutes' time.' Where is one's soul's peace now? And this time it is
the real thing, everyone is racing downstairs with hastily packed

suitcases, rucksacks and miscellaneous parcels. Some people carry their clothes over their arms, and the loudspeaker never stops. The air-raid situation is reported every hour, one listens all the time to that voice from outer space. Usually we just stay in our own cellar, but when the news grows more serious we drag some of our possessions along to the nearest bunker in the Dorotheenstrasse, where a queue of impatient people is already forming by the entrance. No prams or big pieces of luggage are allowed in. If the reason for all this were not so frightful, life as a whole not so hopeless, one could see the funny side of this conglomeration of humanity in this cold, cave-like building, with its hard, narrow benches, its windowless concrete walls. All sorts of people are assembled here. We were squashed between two voluminous females from the Mühlenkamp/Langenkamp district, who made themselves comfortable with cushions, blankets and thick sandwiches and shouted in turn at their children, Rosa and Sylvia, dealing out the occasional clip over the ear. They also embarked on sensational gossip about their coal merchants and mutual acquaintances. 'Watch out, or you'll get a whopper,' poor Sylvia was threatened, because the child was leaning against the chalky white wall. This unfortunate infant, wearing its entire wardrobe of coats and dresses one on top of another, was totally unable to move its arms. Ultimately one has to admire these women. They work all day and still keep their sense of humour. The fat one next to me said she had carried a whole ton of coal, sack by sack, from the depot to her home. Only the last one she had left in a corner for her husband to pick up. For hours and hours they have to stand and queue, as terrible a waste of time as the endless sessions in the bunkers. Our people have limitless patience and perseverance. Our butter ration has just been cut again, three instead of four issues per month, but the only reaction is quiet grumbles and sighs. 'Can you manage?' one asks the other. 'Got to,' is the typical reply, spoken in the broad Hamburg dialect. Our life is so difficult to describe, and for those who have not been through it, hard to imagine. I have just had a talk with Maria, trying to plan a birthday celebration for myself,* which at the same time should be a farewell party for the Hahns. With cutting irony Maria said, 'And what do you suppose I should cook? We've got nothing, absolutely nothing.' She repeated this harsh *nothing* so

---

*Mathilde Wolff-Mönckeberg was sixty-five on 1 April, 1944.

often that in the end I crept sadly out of the kitchen. Towards the end of a ration period there literally is nothing.

But I still foster a little hope. Believe it or not, even I have taken to bartering, as everybody else does, and it really has its fascination. By chance I have got hold of a tobacco ration card and I am holding on to it steadfastly, despite W.'s desire to appropriate it. We even had angry words about it. Margot, Jacoba's maid, who is in the country for the moment, knows where to exchange a piece of fat bacon for it. I'm rather proud and shall proceed. Down below in the cellar is our large dining-room table, which we cannot house here any more. It is getting damp and warped, poor old thing. For many years the Wolff family gathered around it to eat big, wholesome meals. Your stepfather sat at it as a growing lad under the hanging gas-lamp doing his homework in the evenings. I can see him in my mind's eye, a pale, delicate boy, yet with a mature expression, immersed in what he was reading, while his fingers played absentmindedly with his fair, forward-falling hair. I am quite upset about this table, but we cannot afford sentimentality now. I have exchanged the table for fat and meat and quite a number of other delicatessen, which the new owner will bring from her canteen. What else can one do these days? The stomach demands its due and money does not buy a thing. Everyone has oodles of money. Our clothing coupons are supposed to last till the end of the war. When will that be? So there is no temptation in that direction as so often in the old days, and one cannot be extravagant. You can only persuade workmen into your house if you press cigarettes into their hands or treat them to a glass of brandy. The man from the gas board whom I tried to inveigle into letting us have a new cooker, had to be softened with a can of beer, two sausage sandwiches and finally a cigar.

Yet our life is not completely materialistic, concentrated solely on business deals. Never before have I listened to as much beautiful music as during this fifth war winter. We treated ourselves to season tickets for various music cycles and trudged through rain and storm, and even when it snowed like fury, to the 4 p.m. concerts in the Musikhalle. I derived the greatest pleasure from Hans Erich Rübensahm playing Beethoven. He played all the sonatas by heart, five at a time, seeming to be so totally involved that one had to follow with breathless abandon. I had read a Beethoven biography by San Galli beforehand, had prepared myself for each individual sonata and found through the medium of literature a deep musical understanding. Profoundly moved, my imagination conjured up Beethoven himself at the piano. Similar delights were the St John Passion and the Stross Quartet. Once they played the Schubert B flat Trio, which we had listened to so often when Thys brought it for our gramophone, and every note was familiar. More than ever people need to restore themselves with spiritual and artistic gratifications. W.'s public lectures on Shakespeare are packed. The biggest University auditorium is stuffed to capacity with all sorts of people, who, in the old days, would never have dreamed of coming. All the Hamburg Sievekings are present, Frau Blohm, Tante Lili Siemsen, Marianne Eggers and husband, even Jacoba. And it is worthwhile. W. knows, he lives his subject. From the profound depth of his knowledge he recreated King Lear and Macbeth for us. We saw, clearly illuminated, a sharply defined portrait of the bearded old King, searching in bottomless despair and madness through the wasteland, losing his mind, only to find it again ultimately and dying at the highest pinnacle of true consciousness and complete wisdom. That particular lecture W. brought to a close with the words spoken by Edgar : 'Bear free and patient thoughts,' hardly able to master his own tears, and there was an echo in every heart. Another time the grim figures of Macbeth and his Lady appeared before our eyes, the crazed fantasies of this benighted warrior who fears the ghost of Banquo, and his wife, who, in her semi-conscious state cannot wash the blood of guilt from her hands. These too were unforgettable experiences. And in between the everlasting sound of sirens, of anti-aircraft guns, long lists of the fallen, reports of the worst battles of world-history, of diabolical weapons, gas and murder, mud and ice, shot-down planes and sunk warships, detonated old cathedrals, human beings buried alive and charred corpses. In the newspapers we are told of a golden future and *final victory*! All lies, lies!

29 April, 1944. Saturday.
Eleven years ago today Jan returned to Hamburg. W., Ruth, Mimi and I sat in the house in the Gellertstrasse, having just finished supper. Ruth and I had planned to meet his boat the following morning, a Sunday, to see it arrive from the Argentine. Those were the plans – then we heard a car stop, the garden gate open and the

doorbell ring. Ruth ran to the front door, uttered a loud cry and we all followed. And there he was, returned after nine years, the same, yet different, so terribly thin. I broke down when I saw him and folded him in my arms. One realized at once that life had been harsh to him, one could read it in his features, in his dark eloquent eyes, in his clothing. With no overcoat and only a tiny suitcase, this was my truant son. He was not unhappy, on the contrary, he was full of *joie de vivre* and, I believe, full of hope. He describes this reunion in his autobiography, the one I received from Quito after his death, and which I have translated for you from Spanish into German. Today I relive this meeting with him, also the short but wonderful time we spent together from 29 April to 10 August, 1933. After that date we never met again.

I have not written for some time my dear, far-away children : Jella, Thys and little Ruth. Darkness is drawing in on us. We live through a fearful symphony of horror. There is no day, hardly a night without air-raid warnings, we have a new system of public warning of a minor and major kind. Four to five times per day these warnings are announced and many people run to the bunkers at the earliest opportunity, carrying along their treasured possessions. Everybody is afraid, we are all afraid, I am afraid too. My imagination is working overtime. I can hear the landmine which hits our house, can feel it crumble and crash, and then with a fiendish final noise, everything is over. The end is bound to be near, whichever way it comes. People whisper of invasion – but from where and by whom? The Russians have broken through in the Eastern sector, have advanced as far as Galicia; yet of course we are told that our troops have stemmed this penetration, despite the fact that we are withdrawing all the time. Probably you know all this much better than we do. Aerial warfare is increasing daily, nearly all the big towns, many small ones as well and even villages have been attacked. W. is especially sad about Munich, his beloved Munich, which has had very heavy raids. The old Pinakothek has been demolished, also the Residenztheater and the beautiful old Town Hall. We were worried about Tante Ida until her reassuring telegram came. You have no idea how exhausting it all is in the long run. No sooner asleep than the beastly siren goes. We spring out of bed, tear on some clothes, stuff things into a suitcase and rush down in the lift with the luggage, which grows daily because we now have to take provisions too into the shelters. Bulky, puffing people come from all directions, suitcases are piled on top of each other. Even in the cellar we have a loudspeaker, and every few minutes the warning voice drones at us: 'Take care, take care, bombers approaching. Several squadrons of heavy aircraft are advancing towards the city boundaries. Reconnaissance planes are already over the town, bombs have been dropped,' etc. It was child's play during the early years of the war. No one ever thinks of sitting comfortably in a deck-chair with a book now. Our Maria makes for the large bunker in the Dorotheenstrasse at the very first note of the siren. When will it be our turn again? This is the everlasting refrain of our thoughts. It is bound to hit us again, as it did before, the pathetic remains are sure to be demolished, like in Cologne, Essen, Aachen, Frankfurt am Main, Friedrichshafen and many other towns. There are now fifty-nine people in our block of flats, every room is full, billets on all floors and not all as peaceful as in ours.

A dreadful thing happened to Frau Burlefinger's evacuees, a bombed-out family. At 5 o'clock in the afternoon we emerged at last from cellars and bunkers to have something to eat. Nobody was at home except the young son of this family. His parents could not return from town because of the alarms. He was an anti-aircraft cadet, a tall blond boy. When his parents eventually returned, they found him dead on the floor, he had shot himself, whether intentionally or not nobody will ever know. No one had heard anything as we were all downstairs. That very morning I had talked to him.

But now I must tell you about Jacoba and Gustav Heinrich, and that is a long story with many chapters. Ever since those catastrophic raids and our flight to Böckel they have lived in a state of mounting tension, uncertainty and frustration. After that frightful experience, Gustav Heinrich was possessed by one thought only, to get away from Hamburg. He had envisaged this to be much easier than it turned out to be, and after almost a whole year of planning and searching and rejecting it is still virtually impossible. He travelled round the province of Hanover when he was in Böckel, but failed to find a place to live, returning after each journey more tired and desperate than before. New schemes were worked out, hope grew again while he paced restlessly up and down, churning things over in his mind. It was torture to watch him. Finally, having achieved nothing, his expectations and hopes shattered, he went to ground in Lindhorst in his mother's billet, a prey to listlessness and

depression. Fritz is also in Lindhorst, in a foster home with simple
but extremely nice people. There Gustav Heinrich sat in uncomfortable surroundings, fussed over and pitied by his mother, and
gave up making plans altogether. It was a terrible time for Jacoba,
who was alone in Hamburg without domestic help and only the
elderly evacuated couple in her flat. Backwards and forwards she
went between Lindhorst and Hamburg, longing to have Fritz with
her and yet knowing that the present arrangements were the best
for him. For me her presence was an undiluted blessing as always.
In the end Hahn's condition became very worrying and we talked
to Professor Bürger-Prinz, who was prepared to admit Hahn to his
psychiatric clinic in Eppendorf. Jacoba persuaded her husband to
do this and herself took him to Eppendorf. Yet, alas, this was not
the right decision either. Every day he implored her to discharge
him, which really made things extremely difficult for her *vis à vis*
the Professor. But she managed it, the superhuman strength in her
frail body ever victorious. Hahn made several trips to Friedrichsroda and eventually finalized a contract with the owner of a
sanatorium, who wanted him as chief physician, and who offered
him a couple of rooms for his personal use. Once Jacoba went with
him, and although food is scarce in Thüringen and neither of them
really took to the superintendent nor to the immediate surroundings, they agreed that Gustav Heinrich would start on 15 April.
The complicated question of moving arose. They wanted to take
most of their things with them, but keep on the flat in Hamburg,
letting all of it except for one big room for themselves. Again
Jacoba had to carry the entire heavy burden. All the preparations
were made by her, while her husband – as soon as the decision was
made – was assailed by dreadful doubts, regarded Friedrichsroda
as hell itself, living there as banishment and wanted only to stay in
the place he had been so desperate to leave ever since the previous
autumn.

Right up till the last moment he tried to get out of his commit-
ment. On my birthday they both came to a farewell dinner party,
he in the depths of despair. I did not want to be toasted, just to
raise my glass to their future. Tears made a speech impossible.
Thanks to bribery with a bottle of brandy, their furniture had
already gone, also boxes full of books, china and clothes. Their flat
looked deserted and poor Gustav Heinrich paced up and down,
finding no peace. One morning when I went over to them his

despair moved me so profoundly that I wept with him. It was a miracle that he actually departed. Jacoba came and stayed with us. We had looked forward to that, although I could not make it very peaceful for her. She still had lots of things to pack and stow away. I got a dressmaker in to alter some of my frocks for her, and tired or not she had to try them on. She had to look decent at the sanatorium's table d'hôte. But every evening we sat together and read aloud, either Tante Lulu reading Fontane, or W. reading *Tom Jones*. At 10 o'clock we would withdraw to my bedroom and talk without being interrupted. It was lovely to wake up in the morning and find her there. But after only two days Gustav Heinrich telephoned to say that he could not possibly remain in that place. The furniture had already arrived, and we faced new chaos, new despair, new questions, what now? Jacoba rushed around, making endless enquiries, taking counsel from the Medical Association. She spent a whole day in Hagenow, looking at another sanatorium, and foolishly, we began building castles in the air again, how I would visit them, what they would plant in the garden, etc. All for nothing.

25 June, 1944.

The foregoing chapter has to be finished with the words : Gustav Heinrich is dead. Was that not somehow predestined? I will tell you about the inevitability of this tragedy. The last thing I told you was that in no circumstances would he stay in Thüringen. There followed priority telephone calls, telegrams and consultations with the Medical Association, who in the end suggested a hospital in Neustadt on the Baltic Sea. A decision had to be made instantly. Gustav Heinrich returns to Hamburg. Both go to Neustadt and negotiate with the Director of the big hospital, where everything seems to be fairly auspicious. Gustav Heinrich was to be in charge of a department, Jacoba too is offered a part-time position. They are to have two big rooms, can have Fritz with them, and a school is available. G.H. can do a course in obstetrics. The furniture was still in Friedrichsroda, all the ten big boxes have temporarily disappeared, their flat here is empty and very uncomfortable, but perhaps one can hope and take heart. Everything that is at least partly acceptable, however, is quickly devalued in G.H.'s eyes. His one desire remains Hamburg and his own practice. To gain this end he becomes overactive, admits no obstacle, and it is difficult to understand why the Medical Association remains adamant, especially since all his old patients phone and express their wish to have him back. In vain he fights, poor man, running his head against a brick wall. Back in his beloved flat, though empty and desolate, he is content. *He does not want to leave.* I shall never forget his look of hopeless resignation. The day to start his new job comes. Jacoba was going to follow him, still had to see to various details, re-pack what had been taken out of the suitcases. Also Fritz had to undergo a tonsillectomy in Hamburg. So G.H. went to Neustadt but came back at every opportunity, each time more desperate than before. I hoped that all would be well once Jacoba had joined him. She intended to start on 12 June, to rebuild and start afresh.

Fritzchen's operation was a great success, his throat healed quickly and his presence brought joy to us all. He has grown into a strong, healthy boy in Lindhorst. As usual I had to start reading aloud to him again, and we are still the best of friends. Jacoba took him back to Lindhorst for a little while to his foster-parents. She was ready to leave for Neustadt. On Thursday, 8 June, G.H. reappeared in Hamburg with a horrible toothache. He looked ghastly and was completely downhearted. I saw him sitting on the window sill in his big room, staring down into the garden, wrapped in silence. They postponed their departure from Saturday to Monday, because he was so unwell. W. and I went out on Saturday night to have supper with Professor Kroetz. Because of an air-raid warning we were late coming home and didn't get to bed until 2 o'clock. But Jacoba had phoned to say that all was well. At 5 o'clock in the morning she phoned again. 'Mother, my husband is very ill, I think he is going to die.' I was up and out of the house in no time. We advised her to phone Professor Kroetz, who immediately sent an ambulance. Gustav Heinrich was carried downstairs on a stretcher, and Jacoba and I followed him through the grey dawn and the still, bombed-out city to a hospital in Altona. She was offered a bed in the same room and allowed to stay. I went home sadly. He died during the night of Tuesday-Wednesday. He went to sleep very gently and never regained consciousness. There was double pneumonia and his weak heart made recovery impossible. They did everything possible, half-hourly injections, blood transfusions, saline drip. Jacoba never slept at all, and was with him till the end. I went to the hospital every morning. Professor Kroetz was a true friend.

And, almost simultaneously, there occurred the invasion of Northern France, starting on 6 June. An unforgettable day. Ever since those horrifying new missiles, there have been vast battles on three fronts by day and night. Hamburg, too, has had another couple of heavy terror raids. One keeps wondering how it is possible to sustain this crazy existence relatively quietly? But no one ever laughs any more, no one is ever light-hearted or happy. The inner tension is leaving its mark on every face. I can never get to sleep before 1 o'clock, because that is when the siren starts to howl. The remainder of Hamburg has now been destroyed during the two terror raids of 18 and 19 June. The whole of the Mönckeberg-strasse is now in ruins, the church of St Jacobi is burnt out and has lost its spire, and wherever one looks there are signs of new explosions. Again there are hundreds of dead, the population is in flight. We are waiting for the final act.

On the French coast massed enemy forces are advancing slowly under heavy harassment. Many of them never reach land, are destroyed before they get there, while we bombard England's south coast with robot missiles, and they in turn obliterate more and more German and Italian towns. But our newspapers are still full of large victory proclamations. After weeks and weeks of icy cold rain the sun has returned, to peer ironically through the innumerable windowless ruins. The overflowing dustbins exude a foul murky smell, and muck, paper and rotting vegetation cover the streets. But 'everything is going to be restored ever so much more beautifully than before'! Does anybody believe this?

I wish I could have memorized the words W. spoke when we stood by Gustav Heinrich's coffin. Only we three were present, Jacoba, he and I. No music, no clergyman. The coffin stood in the crematorium, covered with summer flowers, candleholders and large vases with multicoloured rhododendrons around it. Jacoba and I sat in the front row. W. stood by the coffin. He said he wished to bid a last farewell to those serious, penetrating eyes, to that quiet voice, to those eloquent healing hands; but not to the intrinsic centre of his being, which would continue to live in us. He then painted a picture of this man, who could not carry existence lightly, who helped so many, but not himself; who managed to commit his span of life to study, to his beloved books, to his family and to his patients; who wanted to carry on unostentatiously and apart from the humdrum of the world, and, when this was no longer possible, who broke under the strain. W. closed by quoting an old oriental text: 'When love is born, the I, the dark despot of one's inner self, dies.'

20 July, 1944.
My little grandson Michael [Goldschmidt] is five years old today. W. is sitting on the balcony in the evening sun just as he did last year, before terror broke loose over Hamburg that night. We are sad. We had a card from Tante Ida's student this morning to say that, while she was away on holiday in Gastein, the flat in the Blüthenstrasse had been gutted. Poor Ida! Just like W., she was so attached to her belongings. They were sacred to her, objects with tender memories of her parents and her youth, and now we too have lost our second home, where we spent such happy holidays for many years and were always made so welcome. Everything is smashed, everything is lost. We have just listened to the news, having acquired our own little wireless set since Jacoba left us a fortnight ago. The public loudspeaker is a nuisance; and we are drenched with news items and hourly bulletins about the danger of air raids. 'Attention please, attention please! Enemy reconnaissance aircraft have been sighted over the district,' in a leaden, droning voice that follows me right into my dreams. Now it is reported in the news that somebody has tried to assassinate 'our honoured and beloved Führer'. The whole of Germany is scandalized by this 'evil' attempt. We know no details as yet.

7 August, 1944.
The seventieth birthday of your father, A. Jolles.
Our little radio is working very well now, since the inspired fingers of Professor Hecke have tinkered around with it. In the middle of the night during a menacing warning we suddenly heard the soothing voice of town councillor Ahrens, 'Uncle Baldrian', as he is called by the population, who has taken over the local radio station and who tells us the situation every hour. We also listened to the Armed Forces Network's report on yesterday's events: terror raid on Hamburg. You poor darlings will also read about it, but once again we were spared. There are still huge conflagrations in the harbour district. Nothing much is left of Hamburg, which is

indeed a ghastly sight. Each new attack tears at one's nerves, one
longs to scream. We have had three consecutive mornings of alarms.
On Friday masses of bombs dropped, Saturday there was nothing,
and yesterday, Sunday, the full onslaught of heavy squadrons. So
far today has been quiet.

I am expecting Jacoba tonight. She is travelling on to Fritz
tomorrow, to pack all his things and then take him via Hamburg
to Neustadt at last. I have been to see her twice already. The first
time we spent two days unpacking all her stuff which was still
stored in boxes, one on top of the other along the corridor of the
hospital. We ran backwards and forwards with all the items, big
and small, which would make her new home more comfortable. It
was odd for both of us, almost like a dream. The hospital is surrounded by a large, derelict park, with a series of allotments and a
yard full of pigs, which are bound to delight Fritzchen. It is all
very peaceful and rural. One can see water, fields and meadows, no
destruction. Her long, large sitting-room has a balcony with flower
boxes, where we had our supper, fairly exhausted. I slept in Fritzchen's bed. On Monday morning I left and she started her new job,
a physician again in a white overall. She felt as if she had been in
a deep dream for eleven years and was waking up in her teaching
hospital. Poor child, I hated leaving her. A fortnight later I went
again and everything was in beautiful order, carpets, pictures, books
and flowers, her own personality imposed on her surroundings. I
know you must be thinking of her, but doubt whether you can
imagine how lost and lonely she is, how all that has happened is
weighing her down. Nor can she discuss it with anyone but me. We
went for long walks through the meadows and along the shore in
the evenings, and we thought of Böckel, the year that has passed
and the ultimately completely unexpected end. Gustav Heinrich
lives in my memory, I can hear his voice, and he and Jan are constantly with me. The 'never again', which this horrible time forces
one to accept in its pitiless reality and which accompanies me
relentlessly in all I do, is so cruel and for me still unimaginable.
There is a limitless tiredness, almost an indifference, and yet one's
nerves are so frayed that at the slightest provocation one just explodes. Thus I find it hard to be kind and patient with dear Tante
Lulu and prefer to be on my own, since I can no longer escape
with all my worries and anxieties to the Klopstockstrasse, where I
found not only physical sustenance – always a cup of coffee and

something tasty to eat – but also a true welcome and real understanding. It was such a relief to me to be with Jacoba, a substitute
for you dear, absent children, and now I am more alone than ever.
The merciless ferocity of all that is happening is without dimension.
And I can no longer speak to you with complete honesty. W. regards
these pages with fear and trembling; he thinks that they could cost
us our lives, send us to perdition. All we can do is wait and *wait,*
and if possible hope. May the Almighty bless and shelter you.

For days on end we have had a harmlessly blue and translucent
sky above us, bringing out the colour of my gloxinias, red and
white, growing in superb stillness on the balcony and hiding the
ruins opposite, to the right and to the left. But in all directions
death and destruction are knotted together, ready to explode. Can
anyone fathom this? I cannot. There is hardly a town still left
intact and yet one becomes indifferent even to these atrocious
ravages, which must be beyond your powers of imagination. For
days we have had no water; everything is chipped and broken and
frayed; travelling is out of the question; nothing can be bought;
one simply vegetates. Life would have no purpose at all if there
weren't books and human beings one loves, whose fate one worries
about day and night.

19 October, 1944.
The ugly, wet brown roads are covered in leaves, big and little,
yellow and red. It is autumn and we are entering the sixth winter of
the war. I have left these pages alone for some time, did not feel
like writing, for one cannot sing the same song over and over again.
The picture of the world has changed quite drastically since 7
August.* Huge armies threaten our frontiers, to the west, south
and east. Only yesterday Himmler made a vociferous appeal for a
people's army, composed of all available males from sixteen to sixty
years of age. Boys of fourteen are already digging defences everywhere, and total war is upon us to such a degree that all theatres
and all concert-halls are closed, and women up to fifty years of age
have to do essential war work. Have we really reached the final and
most frightening phase of this diabolical war? When the invasion

*On 7 August, 1944, the German armies in Normandy launched a desperate
counter-attack. The Fifth Panzer and Seventh Armies were trapped by the
Allies, losing 10,000 dead and 50,000 prisoners.

7   A photograph taken in Hamburg during the bombing raids of July 1943.

8   Hamburg at the end of the war.

9   Hamburg after its surrender. German civilians crowd round a British tank outside the Dammtor Station.

10   Hamburg after its surrender. A food queue.

troops, after initial setbacks in Normandy, broke through and took possession of the whole of France, in next to no time gathering strength at the Dutch-Belgian frontier, we were almost convinced that the end was very near. One question remained, who would swamp us, Russia or the British and Americans? I used to listen to the X radio at a friend's house, and my heart was filled with hope. But now it looks as if we are in for another delay of months, at least weeks. Around Antwerp and Aachen furious battles have raged for days with enormous losses on both sides. Success and defeat alternate. It seems now that the Americans have taken Aachen and Metz. They are fighting for every house, every cellar, every inch of ground. English troops have tried to advance through Holland, so far unsuccessfully. Parachutists, who were landed behind our lines, were annihilated. Step by tiny step they advance, far too slowly for my madly tense and wild impatience. The same is happening in Italy, where there is a desperate struggle to penetrate into the Po Plain. Rumania and Serbia have abandoned us as allies, also poor Finland which has become a Bolshevik country. In the East battles are raging along the whole line; in the northern part the Russians are at the frontier of East Prussia! The background music to all this excruciating fighting and the unimaginable sacrifices of human lives, armoured vehicles, aeroplanes, etc. is the never-ceasing noise of droning aircraft passing across poor Germany, leaving havoc in their wake in cities, villages, station-yards and factories. It must be an absolutely gruesome picture seen from above. The army bulletin gave out today that Kassel, Cologne and Bonn were subjected to very heavy bombing yesterday. In some of our towns only a few houses are left; Münster and Darmstadt and also Cologne and Frankfurt are almost totally destroyed.

We too had renewed terror raids. During the last the University was badly damaged. My poor W. has to do air-raid warden's duty there. He goes every sixth day in the early evening and returns cold and disheartened the following morning. So far the fate of the University and whether the winter term will start have not been decided. Many universities will be closed, some have been amalgamated with others. Our departments of Law and Humanities may be transferred to Göttingen. In every respect this winter is going to be wretched : a cave existence, darkness outside and inside, and not even the consolation of music. But we still have to be grateful to have escaped so far. Our flat is still relatively comfort-

D

able; other women of my age have to do without domestic help and I am quite spoilt with the grumpy bear Maria. Once a week she invites her nice sister from Pinneberg for company. She stays the night with us, helps in the house the next morning with the same circumspection and cleanliness as her not so nice sister. That makes life much easier. I need not bother about the kitchen at all, only do the shopping. And she still manages to put good food on our table without fail. Rations are cut persistently and to eke them out is a problem. One is always hungry, greedy in fact, and would like to eat for hours. I refuse to think of certain dishes and know that I never used to be so materialistic in the past.

I do miss Mimi. My dilapidated underwear cries out for her needle. I am trying to mend sheets as best I can and Tante Lulu reads aloud staunchly. We have started Sorel's recollections of Goethe. My faithful little Mimi does not write very happily but it is impossible to find out what is wrong. She keeps hinting that her niece Therese is unwilling to keep her there, but never a reason why, and she asks me not to mention it in my letters. W. has written a calm and polite letter to Therese asking for information. We cannot contemplate having her back. There are hardly any trains between here and Freiburg, never any in the daytime, and there is the constant danger of dive-bombing. It took a lady three days to get from South to North Germany. She had to wait eleven hours for one train and then it was packed with fugitives. It is difficult to imagine our present dilemma. No permits can be obtained for journeys beyond a certain distance. Neustadt is just within our visiting radius, 93 kilometres away. I have been there four times now and do so enjoy being with Jacoba and Fritz. It is like a haven of peace, although they have just as many alarms. My armchair by the window is so cosy, the mountain of socks and stockings to be darned shrinks, the pages of the book I am reading to Fritz almost turn by themselves, and Jacoba comes, gentle-footed and quiet, always bringing something delectable. We are a happy trio and Fritz suggests that I should stay for ever. Once I was there when a big transport of wounded arrived from Kiel. They were all burn cases, young and old, bundled up and moaning. This was the outcome of that bestial new weapon, the phosphor-poison bomb.

Within a matter of ten days my sister Susi has lost two of her big grandsons, Hans Georg Grote and Gerdt Westphal. Now there are three photos of dead soldiers on her writing desk, for Karl Grote was killed last year. The number of dead grows and grows. Your cousin Amadäus has been missing since May. This is enough for today, I cannot paint a happy picture. As a fitting gesture to the time in which we live, Fritzchen has made an outsize drawing of the first terror raid on Hamburg as a birthday present for his grandfather.

5 November, 1944.

Here I am, with you again. It is a grey, damp, typical November morning. W. and I are alone and very quiet. We have listened to a radio performance of Brahms and Schumann songs and a Schubert quartet. Thys would rejoice if he knew that at long last we have been converted to the wireless. It is still only Jacoba's little set and we use it mainly for the air-raid forecasts. We have got accustomed to the soothing voice of 'Uncle Baldrian'. It always begins : 'And now the air situation report for Hamburg ! Attention, attention ! Fighter planes over North-West Germany ! I repeat !' I do not think we shall ever forget that voice.

I often ask myself what this period of time will look like in our memory. Which particular picture will demand precedence over the others, and will there ever be a time without screeching sirens, without above us the deafening crashes of explosions and within us fear and worry? Just imagine for a moment that during the month of October 1944 – I have just counted – we had thirty-five air-raid warnings and eight heavy bombardments in this town alone. As soon as the siren starts the first warning, we immediately turn on the radio, shove last things into our suitcases, which always stand ready by the front door, fill the bath with water, turn off the gas, and with the second alarm, hurry down into the cellar. This has become completely automatic, regardless of whether it disrupts the day in the morning, postpones our meals for hours, or comes right in the middle of one's first heavy sleep. Last week I was so utterly exhausted that my only desire was for peace. Maria assured me that she was very ill and stayed in bed. We had practically no gas, only a tiny flame which fizzled out every minute. On Wednesday there was no gas at all from 7 o'clock in the morning onwards. We had soaked some haricot beans and I had managed to get a good piece of beef. But what were we to do without gas? Some ten times I went up to the porter's flat to beg a small place on their hospit-

able coal-fired range, but kind Frau Senkpiel was out. In the end I
sent W. and Tante Lulu out to eat in a pub and myself collapsed
on a kitchen chair and drank a glass of icy-cold skimmed milk and
ate two pieces of bread with a speck of butter. We have been
getting ¾ lb. of butter per month per person, but during November
received only 200 gr. for the same period. Then I heard Frau
Senkpiel's familiar step above me and rushed upstairs with my pot-
ful of beans, which she returned at 7 o'clock, steaming hot and
exuding a delicious aroma. Just at that moment, of course, the
alarm sounded and I buried my lovely dish under blankets and
cushions to keep it warm.

W. and I had been to see the von Gosslers in Niendorf that
afternoon. I had gone with an empty stomach, cold and rather
bad-tempered. It was pouring with rain and terribly windy, and
stupidly I was wearing my only pair of decent shoes, also a new
black velvet hat! That is a fabulous acquisition, made from an
evening cape which Hermione once gave to Ruth. My own umbrella
is broken and I had to crouch under W.'s large *parapluie*. Oh, how
angry we both were. We swore we would never go out again during
this hateful time. But a lovely open fire, a cup of real tea, home-
made cakes and such a friendly welcome from dear people restored
our equilibrium, and, wearing my dear friend Nadia's stockings,
existence became bearable again. Back home again, as I have already mentioned, we endured a long session in the shelter before
the all-clear and a devastating longing for the beans and beef.
Another day we went out to tea with the Schlincks, the parents of
Ruth's friend, and sat in their cellar. That's how it is these days.
Tante Vilma was in Hamburg with [her daughter] Marlene for a
week. She did not have a single day without air-raid warnings and
witnessed several heavy attacks on our beloved city. Harburg is supposed to look exactly the same as Hamm and Rothenburgsort [all
suburbs of Hamburg], with 35,000 homeless people and 800 dead.
It must be frightful.

Tante Resi [her sister Therese] communicates only by letter, she
has no telephone and there are no trains. Tante Tido's [her sister-
in-law Clothilde] reports from Bonn are haunting. I will tell you
verbatim what she writes. 'An incendiary bomb hit and exploded
in our air-raid shelter. I was barely able to tear the baby from its
cradle, to push and squeeze the eight children (six grandchildren
and two evacuees) through the blocked entrance. They all clung to

me, screaming. Another incendiary was dropped on the top of the house. Both were extinguished. We had to feed twenty-two people in the house for the next few days, with no gas, no light, no water, nothing except a tiny paraffin stove. We are still nine for every meal.' Countless people are homeless in Bonn. The University and hospitals have been destroyed, the inner city is completely in ruins. No public transport and no mail collection. Your cousin Lilla's husband has been missing for two months but there is just a slender chance that he has been taken prisoner. Your cousin Ricci Berckemeyer is an American prisoner. Everything combines to drive us to desperation, but the illustrious party bosses still blabber of victory, and the new people's army is greeted with enthusiasm.

Forty bomb craters cut through the Hirschpark. An air-mine came down at the corner of Görne- and Heilwigstrasse, demolishing ten houses in one fell swoop. We heard it descend and it sounded like a giant waterfall. It was a terrifying experience. We could hear it approach, nearer and nearer, whining its way down and then crashing with such force that we all cowered on the floor and many screamed. When will it be our turn?

Tante Resi writes from Harburg, 'We have lived through purgatory. At least we have now got light again, and one's demands grow more modest. Harburg and all the surrounding villages have taken a terrible beating. My granddaughter's school received a direct hit. Gisela mended our roof herself! I was terrified to see her antics up there. Just now we have had another short but sharp air attack. We are still alive, but there are huge fires and the light has gone again.'

23 December, 1944.

You are right, my darlings, I must send you a line before Christmas and the end of the year, must unburden my heavy heart to you. Why have I been silent for so long? Because this sixth war winter holds nothing but darkness, kills all initiative to write about it. Everything is so hopeless and there is no point in repeating again and again that one cannot bear it any longer, that patience has come to an end, that it is nothing but 'shit and buggery' as a soldier said, who stood behind me in a queue at the post office. Tomorrow is Christmas Eve and we are sitting here once again—

29 December, 1944.

The beloved siren put an end to my letter-writing activities and chased me down into the cellar. Nothing happened, thank goodness, but I did not feel like writing any more. Now Christmas is over, the old year is running out and the shortest day behind us. Is it possible that it will get lighter again? On the whole we had a good, festive week. Maria disappeared to her sister on the 24th and I enjoyed the absence of her continuous moans and groans, pottered quite happily in my cold kitchen and did what pleased *me* for a change. To be fair, she had pre-cooked our food : a 2 lb. piece of casseroled fillet steak and a huge big pot full of swedes, the only vegetable available. I also discovered a cold rice pudding and some stewed apples. So we were well catered for. But how different everything is from our erstwhile celebrations on 24 December. No hustle and bustle up and down the stairs with packages and parcels, no arranging of presents in the Christmas-room with its specially delicious smell, its piles of coloured paper and string and gifts galore. In those days I had to rush upstairs eventually to wash the grime off my hands and make myself tidy before going to church. This time Tante Lulu and I wandered slowly to the Christmas service at 2 o'clock in the little Eppendorf church. The dark church was warm and cosy, lit only by candles from the big Christmas trees, one each side of the altar, and while we were singing the dear old carols my thoughts escaped to all of you in far regions of the globe.

Back home I brewed us some real coffee – about thirty-five real coffee beans – and we sat down in the library and lit my last four candles. We ate the cake which Maria had regarded as dreadfully meagre, only a couple of pounds of flour, a little milk, $\frac{1}{4}$ lb. of butter, 2 eggs, baking powder and sugar of course. We unpacked the lovely small parcels Tante Ida had sent with lots of kindly thought-out little surprises. She really is unique in this respect. Heaven knows where she finds things, especially now she has lost her home and all her treasured possessions. She never complains and looks at everything with gracious humour. Munich has had devastating terror raids. Hardly any of the buildings W. was particularly fond of still stand. But it is the same wherever one goes : just ruins and dreary mountains of rubble.

Christmas Day was frosty and sunny. W. and I walked to the Uhlenhorster Fährhaus restaurant. There is nothing much left of it except the old conservatory, where the owner has reinstated his restaurant. By 11 o'clock there was a long queue of impatient and hungry people outside. We managed to share a table next to the window with another elderly couple. Service was slow, but worth waiting for. A cup of soup first, followed after a considerable pause by a large trout fried in real butter. Then after an even longer interval we had venison, with red cabbage and potatoes, and finally an ice-cream. Afterwards we wound our way, past considerable obstacles and after an endless wait for the tram, to Niendorf, sat with the von Gosslers around their open log fire and listened to the Christmas Oratorio by Bach, conducted by Günter Ramin. It was lovely, except for the icy journey home.

W. was supposed to do his air-raid warden's duty on Boxing Day, but he returned after only one hour, and we had a comfortable evening together, again with coffee and cake, each of us deep in a book. He is reading a very exciting thriller by Dorothy Sayers to Tante Lulu and me in the evenings. You must imagine us three sitting round the table in his study, enjoying the sight of Christmas apples and fir-tree branches, Tante Lulu and I darning our worn-out clothes. Apples and greenery are Christmas specialities. Food on the whole is very short and none of us look robust any more. Things are so scarce, particularly towards the end of a ration period. We get only $\frac{3}{4}$ lb. of butter per month, hardly any cheese, $\frac{1}{2}$ lb. of meat per month and a very skimpy ration of cereals. There is never even quite enough bread. The other day Tante Lulu and I had dry bread and black caviare substitute for lunch. It looks and tastes like boot polish, although I have never tasted that. Sometimes we find it amusing. Maria can only see the tragic side. Her refrain is forever, 'We have nothing, absolutely nothing.' Sometimes I have an insurmountable longing to eat fatty things, sweet ones too, and have to pinch a spoonful of sugar. This too is in very short supply, and we would have even less if Jacoba did not give us her jam ration when I visit her, so that I can use my card to get sugar alone. She always has things to spare for us, and when I am in Neustadt I feel well. The dear child was supposed to come with Fritz, but was prevented by work; so many people are ill. We cannot go to her for her birthday as we had intended, because she has an inflammation in her leg and has to lie up for a few days. But we can at least communicate by phone.

Our big counter-offensive in the West [the Ardennes, 16-24 December] took us by surprise, and more than ever we ask : What is going to happen to all of us, and when will this insane war be over? It has been comparatively quiet just recently, but western Germany has had the worst battering yet. One shudders to read of the destruction caused by the new weapons and new bombs. Is that still supposed to be human? You must have noticed that I have lost all my former brisk initiative in accounts of our daily life, my *élan*. Only disgust, sickness of heart, fear and horror are left. I am worn out and tired. One becomes insensitive, indifferent, cannot try any more, and sometimes there are hot, bitter, scalding tears. Our Jan has his candle and his evergreen branch, too. There, the siren is screaming again.

Later. Nothing happened, and we had rather a pleasant evening with the Leisers downstairs. He is the owner of this block of flats, a middle-aged, but still crisp, well-preserved and elegant gentleman, with a wife many years his junior, brunette and polite, and a sweet little two-year-old daughter, who adores me. Their small Christmas tree was glowing with lights, and they treated us liberally with strong coffee, masses of Christmas cake and excellent wine from the Saar. As a result the conversation became very lively and Herr Leiser regaled us with all his successful bartering exploits in the nearby countryside, where he has many sources of exchange. In exchange for cigarettes he managed to stock up for Christmas with all kinds of things, including a large joint of pork, a rabbit, eggs and butter. I must say I felt envy rising in me, but W. is neither interested in, nor in favour of such transactions, and having run out of objects to barter, I have had to give up this trade, which was quite flourishing at one time. Frau Leiser is a passionate cook. She became quite dewy-eyed when she talked about her culinary experiments. They are pleasant people. We did not climb up to our flat until after midnight. This morning, 30 December, the army communiqué speaks of a momentary lull in the big battle in Belgium and of street-fighting in Budapest. Slowly, very slowly the year is rolling to a halt, the last few days drag on. There is no news from Mimi, only daily postcards from Ida. She is remarkably serene and unvindictive. A huge yellow moon looks down on our devastated city.

1 January, 1945.
There, the New Year. Now we find renewed courage. It is just as
well that we cannot lift the veil that hides 1945.

18 January, 1945.
The new year's first gift was profound sadness. On 8 December our
darling Mimi died. She contracted bronchitis, as in every winter,
but neither Jacoba nor I was there to nurse her. Twice we had
literally torn her from the arms of death. A frightful terror raid on
Freiburg on 29 November was obviously too much for her. She
went to sleep in a hospital that had been evacuated. Only a couple
of days ago I received a letter, dated 17 December, from her great-
niece, Frau Gertrud Schmidt, daughter of Frau Therese Schweizer,
announcing the death of her 'dear little grandmother' as she calls
her. For weeks we had been without news and were very worried.
I wrote several letters and sent money, but had no acknowledge-
ment. And now she is gone, gone for ever.

All this sounds so cold and stark, but I just cannot believe that I
shall never see her again. At every step I feel she is with me, I see
her dear, kind face, watch her busy activities : she is darning by
the window; she is behind the sewing machine; she is kneeling on
the floor dusting; she is brushing carpets; she is down the road
fetching milk; always eager to help, always meticulously neat and
tidy. And has all this really come to an end? Will I never be able
to talk with her about things in the past, about 'our' children,
giving you all your childish pet-names? When we were alone
together we had no greater joy than going back over old times in
Freiburg, Wannsee, Gross-Flottbeck and finally the Gellertstrasse.
We laughed about our many small disagreements, which always
ended in conciliatory tears and bound us together more firmly than
before. For you it is as if the frame which held your childhood so
tenderly together has shattered and burst, as if for the first time
you are truly alone and adult, blown out in all directions into a
hostile world. Her trusting love still held you together as a little
group and right up to the last she would end each letter in her fine
stiff handwriting : 'I am always thinking of you and the "little
ones".' I feel so awful that she died alone, none of us present, not a
single loving word from us, that the final year of her life was so
sad and lonely. I blame myself for letting her go, for not fetching

her back. But that was impossible. We took such careful counsel with Jacoba before she went, hoping she would return after a few months, cancelled her registration only temporarily, and were convinced that a spell of rest with her niece Therese would do her good, that she would have more peace there than with us. Who could have known that this woman, whom I remembered to be a friendly and tidy person in the old days, would be so unkind to her elderly aunt? We could never find out what happened. Dear Mimi wrote rather confused little letters, hinting that she was not very happy, that she felt rather unwelcome. But when I enquired of Therese what was amiss, I never had a reply. W., because I asked him to, sent a letter asking politely, but urgently for information. Nothing but silence. Apparently she tore up all our letters without having read them. Meanwhile things got worse here, became more and more unbearable. At last a very charming letter came from this great-niece, Frau Schmidt, telling me that Mimi was with her family, but that she was not at all well. She was indignant about the treatment Mimi had received, almost wished down a terror raid on Therese, and this indeed happened.

4 February, 1945.
It is Sunday. I am all alone in the flat, which is quiet, dark and cold. W. is on duty at the University. He went after an early lunch at 1 o'clock, and will not be back until tomorrow. Tante Lulu has gone to [her daughter] Fanny for tea. Since I have no flour coupons to spare and did not want to eat their cake just like that, I preferred not to go with her. I rather like being alone. I slept a little on W.'s couch in his den, which is the warmest room. I brewed a cup of tea from a few tea leaves and have eaten a stale bun. I have read a good short story by Stefan Andres, called 'We Are Utopia'. Then it was 5 o'clock and time for the army communiqué. Now I am sitting at the desk and will come to you. All these bits of trite news contain a whole world of sadness, a veritable inferno of it.

This sixth winter of the war cannot be compared with anything that went before; previous winters now appear almost bright and light in comparison. The enemy is advancing on all fronts, West, South and East, and has broken through our frontiers in many places. 'We are slowly but surely being strangled,' Tante Tido writes from Bonn. I doubt whether there is a single undamaged city in the whole of Germany and most of them are sad ruins. If one had a bird's-eye view, one would see nothing but devastation, destroyed railway-lines, fields torn open by craters, burning factories and hordes of fleeing human beings. A never-ending stream of fugitives is rolling from the East towards Berlin and Hamburg. When they arrive, after days of toil in open farm carts through ice and snow, babies frozen to death at their mothers' breasts, more bombs are showered on top of them. It is unbelievably wretched and frightful. We are still comparatively fortunate, but for how much longer? Hunger knocks at every door. New ration cards are to last for five weeks instead of four, and no one knows if they will be issued at all. We count out potatoes every day, five small ones each, and bread is becoming more scarce. We are growing thinner and thinner, colder and colder and more and more ravenous. My poor W. is nothing but skin and bones, looks old and gaunt. But one should not talk of oneself during this period of vast, general distress, of certain extinction. Five early warnings, three proper air-raid alarms make a day like yesterday typical of the time we live in. It started at 10 o'clock in the morning, and immediately afterwards came the real thing, which meant a general exodus to the bunkers. I was on my way to the post office with a letter for Jella, which, thank heaven, was still accepted. On my way back I met the first cavalcade of people, laden and burdened with their belongings like emigrants. There were two little children with large bags round their necks and rucksacks, clutching their dolls; old women stumbling and trembling with fear, carrying their goods and chattels; younger women, heavy loads over their shoulders and on their backs, pressing wrapped-up babies against their breasts, couples hugging bundles of bedding between them; everyone was pushing and shoving towards the dark gate of the bunker. It was laughable and one could have cried. I raced home and up the stairs – the lift has stopped working – put on two frocks and stuffed what I could lay my hands on into my suitcase. Then there was another warning! It is the same today, no respite. One gets so tired, so cold and is always hungry.

18 February, 1945.
A fortnight ago I wrote the following poem for our beloved old Mimi.

Snow-covered grave, I visit you in spirit
And kneel to say a grateful last farewell
To her who was my oldest closest friend.
Would I had had the chance to close your eyes,
Hold in my living arms your dying frame.
Gladly I would have led you to that threshold,
Which like a child you feared to contemplate,
But which, once passed, holds only light for you,
And blessings everlastingly deserved.
Yet here I kneel, my children are beside me
Mourning your loss, joining their gratitude.
We are impoverished without your love
Which generously you bestowed on all my kin,
Children and children's children all alike,
Unfailing source of fortitude and faith
You laughed and suffered with us selflessly.
We wandered side by side for forty years
Through life's long labyrinth of stress and joy,
Clung to each other when grim danger threatened,
Hard work and poverty brought near defeat.
But you remained true to yourself and us.
The hurt is keen, since we grew old together,
That fate did not permit a gentler parting.
You were the link which tied the grown-up children
With days gone by, past treasure's memories.
Now for the first time are they wholly adult.
As long as you were there they still returned
Like infants for a plaster or a kiss
To heal imagined woes or real pain.
You saw the early miracle of smiles,
First tears and temper tantrums, met the storms
Of disappointments, tragedy and hurt
Which later followed with accepting love
And held the balance with your simple trust.
We watched and feared together for their safety
And shared the blissful pride of their success.
The pet-names of the nursery remained
Your property, your lap was always sought
By young and old when needing love from you.
And then the children's children soon became

Another source of care for your indulgence,
They also joined the ranks of your dependents.
Because you gave so much, so generously
Without a selfish thought, richness was yours.
Your place in our hearts, beloved friend,
Is well secured and will for ever be.
Your faith, your trueness, your unending care
Is the example of our future lives,
And I, the oldest, have to try and warm
My lost and lonely soul in thought of you.
This point in time, not blessed with care and kindness,
Leaves only dread and fearful desolation.
The memory of you will keep us going,
If all else fails, your picture will remain.

28. 1. 1945.

Our days are such that one has to drag oneself through the dark, hungry hours, constantly repeating to oneself that there are thousands worse off, all those refugees who had to leave their homes, travel through ice and snow with their children, who die of exposure and land somewhere with *nothing* to call their own. All accounts defy belief. The sick and old are loaded onto farm carts, so are women who have just given birth, and some poor blighted creatures are delivered en route, their infants dying the moment they are born, being put into a box and thrown into the river. In the province of Stormarn alone, 24,000 fugitives had to be billeted out, eight to ten people in one room, sixty in a barn. The spectre of starvation looms over us all. The last bomb-attack on Berlin was the worst our capital has ever had. [Her niece] Lise Schmidt wrote as follows. She had gone shopping in the centre and, when it started, took refuge in the air-raid shelter of a jeweller's shop. When she emerged, the house with the shop was no longer there, only a heap of rubble and a sea of flames. In order to get back to Dahlem, she had to climb over debris and skirt fires for four hours. A thousand dead were counted during that one afternoon. Dresden too has virtually disappeared from the earth, so has Weimar, with the houses of Goethe and Schiller. Not a town has been spared and soon Germany will cease to exist altogether.

I do not suppose that you have the faintest conception of what is happening. But one gets used to it slowly, the constant and everlasting air-raid warnings and the growing emptiness of the stomach. Cold and hunger are bad companions. You become dull, you lack energy and try to lose yourself in sleep. I should love to be more active, but I just haven't any strength left. W. was supposed to give a lecture in Lüneburg last week, but came back the following morning without having attained his purpose. He had had a difficult journey, and just as he was about to start the siren went. He had to go into the shelter, remaining there for so long that the lecture had to be cancelled. Every sixth night he does guard duty at the University from 5 p.m. to 8 a.m. with two other men and two girls. It was almost impossible to provide him with sandwiches. If they are lucky, they warm up a little cabbage. How good it will be when I can tell you something really pleasant again.

The most joyful days were those recently when I received two letters via Jella, one from Mynie [Hermione] and one from Ruth. Both contained photographs; Thys with his two boys, and one of Rhysi and Anna. Moments like that outweigh much of my longing and waiting. Arnold and Rhysi are such big boys already, and little Anna is the image of Ruth. The impossibility of reaching them through all this undiluted horror drives me quite crazy. I can almost see them, feel them, hear them – and yet there is this barrier. Only in my dreams can I sometimes do that. And then I read Goethe's poem from the *West-Östliche Divan*.

> *Ist es möglich! Stern der Sterne,*
> *Drück' ich wieder Dich ans Herz!*
> *Ach, was ist die Nacht der Ferne*
> *Für ein Abgrund, für ein Schmerz.**

I am almost obsessed with this cycle of poems and find in it the greatest treasures. The poem I quoted is one of the most beautiful in the world. Whenever I listen to Beethoven, I cry. Everything wells up inside me and all my dead stand around me : Jan, little Mimi, Jasper and Henki. It is very hard to hold on to a moment in time, as Goethe urges, to capture it and make use of it. To do this

---

*From 'Buch Suleika', *West-Östliche Divan*. Translation :
          Do I press you, star of heaven,
          Truly to my heart again?
          Oh, the night of separation
          Brought the very depth of pain.

one would have to create something that uplifts and transcends. Thank heaven there is beauty *per se*, imperishable and eternal in this gruesome world. The achievements of sculpture and architecture – they are all gone!

6 April, 1945.

Another long silence. Horror is crowding in on us. W. and I are sitting in the kitchen, the only warm room in our flat. They have turned off the central heating a fortnight ago, and it is miserably cold both inside and outside. We never get out of our overcoats these days, and our noses and hands are permanently red. The newspapers said yesterday that gas will definitely be rationed from now on. We are advised to eat in restaurants or to fetch our meals from the N.S.V., the soup-kitchens! It was bad enough having two days without gas, although very often there was none on the days in between. We have no electric light on Wednesdays, but that is not so bad as the days are getting longer, the only positive item in our present misery. Everywhere little green buds dare to brave the light, even on the ruins there are signs of defiant greenery. This spring is a greater miracle than ever. Hamburg was again subjected to severe punishment during these past few weeks, especially Harburg and the harbour, and we counted eight more heavy terror raids. I was caught in one on the open street. I was on my way to Altona to get a permit to travel to Neustadt, when I and lots of others had to leave the train at the Sternschanze because of an air-raid warning. There was a huge crowd trying to get into a bunker, so we decided to walk to the Dammtor Station and set off, despite the fact that we could hear threatening noises in the distance. And then hell broke loose above us. We just managed to reach the open door of the Wilhelmgymnasium; there was no cellar. There were about twenty of us. Stick after stick of high explosives came hurtling down, and we crouched on the floor in a corner, clutching our heads. It was a most extraordinary sensation of totally concentrated fear of death. All the windows were blown in, the walls shook and we waited for the end. I had just one thought in my head : 'How ghastly for all my loved ones never to know where I perished,' and tears were streaming down my cheeks. The woman next to me was kneeling and saying her prayers, screaming for Jesus to help her. But the infernal din went on,

worst of all the swishing noise of the descending bombs, not knowing where they would explode. I ran home on foot afterwards and
my W. and I fell on each other's necks and sobbed. He was nearly
crazy with worry.

One cannot plan anything, for the raids are totally unpredict-
able. They occur in all weathers, sometimes just warnings but then
bombardments five times a day, and always for hours at a time. In
the morning work just has to be left, and then, without gas, we
might eat at 3 p.m., famished and dead tired. We feel a physical
dread of being driven to the very limits, and that our poor Germany is being squeezed out of existence. In the east the Russians
have taken Ratibor and Glogau, are entrenched outside Vienna
and Breslau. In Küstrin they fought street by street. In the west
the Americans have rushed across our frontiers in the past few
days, and many cities are already occupied. When will they reach
us? It is soul-destroying to wait, day and night, for the inevitable
disaster.

It was heavenly to have an unbelievably quiet week in Neustadt
recently. Getting there was rather bad, the train packed to capacity
and still more people pushing in with big pieces of luggage. We
were late, of course, but I arrived alright with my legal travel
permit and Jacoba's new home is charming. She has two rooms,
one a large corner one, in the staff house and Fritz has his own
airy bedroom. We are worried about Fritz. He has developed
glandular tuberculosis since January, when W. and I spent three
days in Neustadt. I found him comfortably installed on the couch
in the sitting-room and in good spirits. His temperature has been
normal for some time, he has a fantastic appetite, but the gland on
his neck is still very swollen. He was thrilled to see his old grandmother, and I to see him. Jacoba made me sleep in Gustav Heinrich's big bed in Fritz's room, and the boy's regular breathing,
combined with the peace up above, gave me tranquil repose.
Miraculously, Neustadt has been spared so far, despite the fact that
there is a training centre for U-boat cadets there. One can hear
the siren in the distance when there are raids on Kiel. The weather
was so mild and beautiful that I was allowed to take Fritz out
for an hour each day. We went to the wood nearby and looked
for the first spring flowers. We picked lots of anemones and
Fritzchen crept under all the bushes to find the first violets.
To my delight he is as fond of flowers as I am, can arrange them

beautifully with gentle, deft fingers in all kinds of vases and pots. They veritably stuffed me with food, which I enjoyed in the company of the children. I left very reluctantly after eight happy days.

20 April, 1945.

And now we have to face the final catastrophe. American troops have advanced as far as Harburg, and the gunfire rolls across our city like thunder. What we have gone through during these past few days you will never be able to imagine. Ultimate calamity haunted every step we took, continuous tense excitement, dashes for the radio to catch up with the latest of more than a thousand different rumours, warnings and alarms alternately from morn till night, and night till morning, and in between, in the short pauses for breath, a race to the shops to purchase newly-released items, together with masses of other people who queue for hours and who are equally tired, worn out and constantly endangered by dive-bombers. We three, Tante Lulu included, are almost skeletons. I have never looked like this before and view my body with disgust, shivering in my shrivelled skin. Hamburg has become a fortress. Wherever one looks there are absurd barricades across the streets between heaps of rubble, to be surmounted by little stone steps, which look as if they have been made by children for fun! Are they supposed to keep us safe? Hamburg people laugh and shrug their shoulders. 'Uncle Baldrian' talks to us every night with his deep bass voice, repeating the reassuring litany that our municipal authority will look after us, that we already have proof of this in the issue of extra rations, a welcome bonus of 100 gr. coffee, 50 gr. tea, 2 lbs. of sugar and ½ lb. of margarine. Apart from this we are told to collect our rations for the 75th period in flour, fat and sugar, and to store them away for emergencies. The rhythm of our lives has changed completely, as we cannot cook and Maria is dependent on the porter's solid-fuel range, has to take her turn with her cooking pot along with the others. Accordingly we have a frugal lunch with three, sometimes four pieces of grey bread, a little fish-paste, cheese when available, and boot-polish caviare. We never get anything hot into our impatient insides before 7 at night. We have no more fuel except old boxes which Maria splits furiously into small bits of firewood. There is no gas at all and electricity only three times a week. We have to cope with that as best we can and are still much better off than others.

Every morning drowsy figures, cluttered with belongings, emerge from the bunkers. Scared to death, they prefer to doss down in that foul air rather than stay at home. I was out at 7 o'clock this morning to queue for deep-frozen vegetables, and being one of the first I managed to obtain three packets of apple-sauce. There was an early-morning freshness about us as we huddled together outside the small cellar shop at the Langenkamp, and almost automatically fell into conversation. All these women looked tired and shared the ardent desire for a rapid conclusion of this horrendous war. There was no hope of victory, not the tiniest indication of hero-worship for the Nazis. *Insane,* they called the whole thing, *criminally insane.* Most of them had had tragic experiences, all of them were longing for peace and the resumption of a normal, quiet existence. No sooner was I home at 9 o'clock, and having just excavated the thermos-flask of milky, sugarless coffee substitute from beneath its cocoon of cushions and blankets in the corner of the sofa, having just drawn back the curtains in W.'s bedroom and laid the breakfast, than the siren goes! That was the first alarm and from then on nothing but disruption. Tante Lulu went out to queue for candles and Maria for sugar, and one warning and all-clear succeeded another.

On 14 April we had another very heavy raid in the night without any warning. It was infernal, especially when one had just come to the surface of consciousness after a deep sleep, tortured into awareness by crashes and clatter. Walls shook and windows rattled, and I was so shocked and frightened that I could hardly get my clothes on. Maria was yelling in the next room; she banged about like a mad woman and raced down the stairs without shoes. I pushed my nightie into my knickers, tore a frock over my head and a coat on top and also made for the stairs. Strange apparitions were assembled in the cellar in the most primitive get-up. This hell lasted only for ten minutes, but how great was the damage! Air-mines and bombs had exploded all round the Dammtor Station, the Alsterterrasse was virtually non-existent, one vast heap of smouldering and burning rubble. W. and I went to have a look at Jacoba's flat and in the whole of the Klopstockstrasse there was not one window left. The main University building was a windowless cavern, the houses opposite were all down, the English department also minus panes of glass, with doors blasted out, and even W.'s table-top was torn off its legs. It is the same picture in the Johns Allee, Mittelweg and Badestrasse. Big blocks of flats are demolished, collapsed like houses of cards, but with a good deal more noise. The din must have been hellish and the conflagration abysmal. My poor cousin Annie Stamann, sister of Tante Lili, was buried beneath her house and was found only three days later. My only surviving aunt, ninety-year-old Tante Adele, died in this night of horror. W. and I had to trudge on foot of course, no trams, and we swayed along arm in arm, like two senile lunatics, tired to death and depressed beyond words. Jacoba's flat looks awful. One of the inside walls has collapsed down the staircase, and windows and doors have been blown out by the blast. Poor Herr Schwarzkopf only had time to throw himself out of bed and onto the floor, when the light went out, thunderous pressure caved the window in, and he lay covered with splinters and flying debris.

I wonder if your children and your children's children will one day be interested in reading all this? For us it is unbearably terrible, as the wear and tear of the past six years weighs us down like the heaviest of nightmares. There is a rumour going round tonight that Hamburg will be declared an open city. If only it were true!

26 April, 1945.

Days and nights drag on their weary way. We are now besieged by the British. Their positions are along Stade, Harburg, Buxtehude and Horneburg, and every now and again we can hear artillery fire, a hollow, angry sound. We thought at first it would happen much more quickly; our resistance, however, is strong, and the entrenchments and barricades around our city are more effective than anticipated. While the Americans have conquered most of the Middle and South Germany – there is hardly a big town not yet occupied by them – the British and Canadians have come to a stop around Bremen and Hamburg, and our torment of waiting goes on and on. All day long we still have warnings and alarms, but Hamburg itself is left in peace except for reconnaissance planes which circle above us with their dark humming noise. Our fighter planes continue to engage the enemy over the coast of Holstein, over Kiel, Neumünster and Oldesloe. In our city centre life goes on amid the ruined, hardly recognizable streets. Endless queues of tired women stand in front of the food shops from 7 o'clock in the morning onwards. They bring little camp stools and wait their turn with hopeful tenacity, only to be told instead that what they yearned to buy has just been sold! It's the same story outside the clothes and shoe shops, since we are supposed to be no longer rationed. There is no point in even trying. One cannot get soap, and we are not allowed to use the iron, so doing the laundry is a mounting problem. A little woman still washes W.'s shirts, but they have only been dragged through water and not ironed. Maria, like Cassandra, forecasts disaster if we use too much electric current, since every evening 'Uncle Baldrian' tells us of the dire consequences of using an excess of electricity. We run the risk of being cut off altogether in our district and would not be able to listen to the wireless any more. Thus we sleep between unironed sheets, and why not? I rinse out my smalls in a tiny drop of warm water. By law our bath has always got to be full of water, because there may also be a water stoppage. Our own personal cleanliness is suffering accordingly.

Herr Leiser, our landlord, came twice last night spilling out frantic new rumours which he had got from the Western Army communiqué. Rosenberg is said to have fled; Göring to have been dismissed because of his heart-disease; Italy to have capitulated, at least the Po front has collapsed. Circumstances in Berlin must be horrifying, with bloody street fighting everywhere, even in the Underground. But Hitler is still there and a few crazy fanatics still believe in victory. There is said to be no water in Berlin and the dead and wounded are left lying in the streets and on public places in their hundreds. The Russians are surrounding this vast metropolis and what has not been destroyed in innumerable air attacks is being shelled and burnt to the ground. The end of the ordeal is near and our imagination is working overtime trying to take in all this horror. What has never happened before in my life is that days are too long for me and I don't know what to do. It is a barren existence which I cannot fight. All the poems which sustained me before are as rigid and dead as I am myself. Only little Ingrid downstairs gives me life and warmth.

There was an announcement just now. Berlin's inhabitants have been driven into a small space in the centre, surrounded on all sides.

1 May, 1945.

I am trying to write with chilblains on my fingers, shivering with cold in W.'s unheated study and wearing a winter coat and fur stole. And this is supposed to be May! The wind is howling outside, the rain pouring down and from the distance come the sharp reports of enemy artillery. We are told that they are going to leave Hamburg to one side, will make for Lübeck. The British have extended their bridgehead near Lauenburg and have reached the Elb-Trave canal. I am terribly relieved that the British, not the Russians, will occupy Neustadt. Within the part of my mind that is not inert and frozen, I had been very much afraid. Just now it was reported on the radio that the defence of Berlin has been reduced to a tiny spot in the very centre. Apart from that the whole city is nothing but a vast area of burning ruins. Mass conviction now spells out only one thing: we have lost the war. Every evening Herr Leiser brings us more unhappy news from the Western Army communiqué. The day before yesterday W. went down with him and didn't return until 3 a.m. He rushed into my room and woke me up with the words, 'It is *over, all over*!' Can you imagine what these words mean to us? After six long years of ever-increasing deprivation, ever-mounting anxiety, of unbelievable losses, just a brief 'over'. However much we strain with every nerve of our beings towards the downfall of our government, we still mourn most deeply the fate of our poor Germany. It is as if the final bomb hit our very soul, killing the last vestige of joy and hope. Our beautiful and proud Germany has been crushed, ground into the earth and smashed into ruins, while millions sacrificed their lives and all our lovely towns and art treasures were destroyed. And all this because of one man who had a lunatic vision of being 'chosen by God'. May he and his followers be caught in just retribution.

The Duce Mussolini, that inflated buffoon, has already been executed in Milan. I do not suppose he ever dreamed that his unburied corpse would be on view in the street, when he boasted with presumptuous bombast to be master of the whole world's fate together with his Axis friend, Hitler. Himmler, it is rumoured, has offered a peace treaty to the United States and England and received the reply that he would have to capitulate to Russia as well. Our army despatches are getting shorter and shorter. Air-raid warning forecasts have ceased. Soon the final decision will come. When one recalls Hitler's flaming victory speeches, his prophecies

and inflated promises that all would be well in the end, one can
only regard our present situation as the quintessence of irony in the
whole history of the world. It serves him right. But we will never
get over this bloody calvary. We have grown old and weary to
death. One sits and searches one's brain for an explanation. The
innumerable giant battles, the endless marches across the length
and breadth of Europe, the invention of fiendish weapons – an
excrescence of the human brain – the hundreds of nights beneath
the terror of bombs which rained from the sky, the sinking and
exploding of valuable and lifegiving equipment in the way of food
and building materials on ships destined for the bottom of the sea,
the blowing up of tanks, shooting down of aircraft, scorched
earth, what was the point of it all, what rhyme or reason was
there for this desperate, ruinous destruction? Was it just a satanic
game?

6 May, 1945.
It is Sunday and I almost hesitate to put pen to paper. Too much
has happened in the few days since last I wrote. The whole world
has changed and part of the crushing nightmare that oppressed us
for so long has been lifted during these five days. I have listened
quite openly to an American and to a British radio station, no
longer threatened with the death sentence for this. I can go along
the road and proclaim loudly, 'Adolf Hitler, the most evil criminal
in the world,' and nobody will tell me to shut up. Can you
imagine that? And can you picture our Andreasstrasse full of
English trucks and private cars; on the pavements and in the front
gardens a milling crowd of English soldiers – and it is a Welsh
regiment, Ruth dear. They serenely patrol the district : one is sitting
in the middle of the road playing with a dog, another one is playing a recorder on a balcony; a couple tumble in and out of the
house, for downstairs a captain has moved into the bottom flat.
What a lot of coming and going! And all this has happened since
1 May, 1945. On the day when I last wrote, shivering with cold –
and the weather is the one thing that has not changed – we had an
announcement in the evening. It was rather sudden. A voice came
over the radio : 'Attention, attention, there is going to be an important and serious announcement for the whole German people.'
The four of us, W., Tante Lulu, Maria and I, gathered excitedly

round the little set in my bedroom. There was preparatory music
from the 'Flying Dutchman' and then a slow movement from a
Bruckner symphony which nearly drove W. to distraction. He
called it 'fruitless whimpering' and could hardly bear it. Then
again, 'Stand by, attention,' and a deep voice said, 'Today* in
Berlin Adolf Hitler died a hero's death at his army post.' A further
bulletin followed telling us that Admiral Dönitz had been nomi-
nated as his successor and would carry on the struggle, following
the Führer's example. We were stunned, having expected news of
the capitulation, and foresaw the final act in Hamburg's history.
Maria wiped away a tear for her Führer. Since the 'whimpering'
drowned out all other news, W. and I went down to the Leisers and
received confirmation of our news from foreign radio stations.
'Adolf Hitler is dead,' blared out at us constantly. Some said he
had shot himself; others that he had had a stroke. One will probably never know the truth. Himmler's proposals for capitulation
have been accepted, but only by America and England. Tired and
disheartened we go up to our flat. Hamburg will suffer the same
fate as Berlin.

The following afternoon, 2 May, Maria bursts into my room.
'Quick, quick,' she shouts, 'we must get provisions at once, hundreds
of people are queueing up already. The British Army is coming at
5 o'clock.' We do not believe her, but go down nonetheless to get
bread and butter if we can. There are great masses of people
everywhere and the air is thick with rumour and supposition.
Lübeck has been taken. After supper Frau Leiser comes dashing
up the stairs, completely out of breath. We must come down at
once and listen to our Gauleiter Karl Kauffmann. Everybody *must*
listen, the windows should be open so that people in the street can
also hear. Down we go and there is 'Uncle Baldrian' introducing
Karl Kauffmann. Our Gauleiter, who has always treated Hamburg
citizens decently, is obviously deeply moved, speaks simply and
with dignity. He does not wish to shoulder the responsibility of
exposing the population, particularly the women and children, to
almost certain death. He is following his heart's dictate and his
conscience and *declares Hamburg an open city.* We will be occupied by the British, all he wants is peace, and he expects perfect
discipline from everybody. This decision will probably cost him his

*Hitler in fact committed suicide on the previous day, 30 April, 1945.

life. Ribbentrop has been replaced by Graf Schwerin-Krosig, who also makes a speech. Where are all the other Party members? Himmler, Goebbels, Göring? Deep silence.

The English transmitter announces that the entire battle-front in the South has capitulated. Berlin's fate is sealed, God knows how many hundred thousands are dead and wounded! Our emotions are very divided. On the one hand there is satisfaction that retribution has caught up with our hated oppressors, that they will have to face punishment for all the unspeakable damage they have caused, for their diabolical machinations and their false triumphant boasts about their enemies. On the other hand there is profound relief that we are likely to become free human beings again, released from our bondage of terror, no more bombs, no bunkers, no hiding in cellars, no sleepless nights, no panicky packing of suitcases. And thirdly there is ineffable sadness, which outweighs all the rest, about our truncated, tortured and tormented fatherland, our Germany, which will no longer belong to us; and our once so proud and happy free Hamburg, which will have to submit to English rule. No wonder sleep does not come, with these thoughts circling in one's head, giving no respite. One spark of happiness cannot be suppressed : perhaps after all I shall see my children again! How much I have doubted this of late I am beginning to realize only now!

On 3 May everybody has to be off the streets by 1 o'clock. Shops and public buildings are closed, public transport at a standstill. They arrive at 3 p.m. Out here we do not notice much. The roads are deserted, not a soul in sight and all is quiet. Towards evening we hear some traffic in the Sierichstrasse. The British Commander of Hamburg gives his first bulletin. That seems very strange and rather sad. 'Uncle Baldrian' is gone, silent. I'm afflicted by a migraine, lie down and feel I never want to see or hear anything again. W. goes down to the Leisers in the evening and comes back with the news that Berlin has been taken, Queen Wilhelmina has returned to Holland, that the British are in Denmark. On Friday, 4 May, we still have the same uncanny silence, but suddenly there are British soldiers everywhere, creeping like ants through the streets, and soon cars, motor vehicles, motor bikes, tanks and armoured cars follow. They settle in, bringing wooden posts with notice-boards : Army Post Office, Tailor, Leave Centre, etc. Lots of people are bursting with curiosity, stand on their balconies all day long and watch what is happening. We decide to keep ourselves busy carting things back up from the cellar, all the things that have been stored there for six years. I brush out W.'s suits, clean out drawers, sort letters and photos in my desk. It is all like a dream, still utterly unreal. In the evening there is the first proclamation by General Eisenhower: we will be able to leave our houses again tomorrow morning at 9 o'clock, and at 10 all the shops will be open. Schools and other educational establishments will remain closed. The Nazi Party has ceased to exist! We go to bed early. It is still cold.

12 May, 1945.

I am wearing my black and white summer frock again, because suddenly summer has come, hot summer, blue sky and a veritable explosion of rich, colourful blossom. We spend almost all our time on the balcony, watching the English soldiers paddling and punting along the canal. They bring a new world of sounds, not all beautiful, to us who have lived so long without cheerful whistling and singing.

I have just looked through this thick manuscript, wondering *when* I will finish it. Not until I can hold you physically in my arms again. Only then can I put the last full-stop after the last word. And re-reading some of these pages I could not fathom, could not appreciate that everything has suddenly changed. W. says that throughout the grim eternity of the war years we constantly prepared ourselves and worked for this, but what presentiment was there during that time of horror and fear? Within a single week all those scoundrels, all those foul-mouthed rascals have disappeared, some dead presumably, some taken prisoner, and Germany has been divided into four zones, an English, an American, a French and a Russian one. Heaven be praised that we do not belong to the last. Dresden and Berlin in Russian hands! Hundreds of thousands of German soldiers in Russian captivity! My thoughts cannot remain still at any particular point. I am revelling in the warmth, the undisturbed nights and the hope for a reunion with all of you. I am already so much nearer to you, my Ruth, since I hear English spoken all around me. W. is very busy with University committee meetings and I sincerely hope they will nominate him as Pro-Rector. The new University Senate is composed of a caucus of like-minded people, and ideally it would be right and proper if the old and the new spirit could rise above the destruction. Sometimes I hope against hope that from the little that is left new treasures will grow, for the good and the useful have survived. In its extinction all the boasting glitter of false metal will make room again for the true light of unalloyed honesty.

13 May, 1945.
During these glowing, hot early summer days I feel the need again and again to come to you, my children. I have just listened to the thanksgiving service from St Paul's in London and almost imagined I could hear you singing, darling Ruth. Yes, you have every reason to sing 'Now thank we all our God'. We, the less fortunate, have to stand aside and swallow our tears. Last night on the radio they gave us an overall picture of the past fortnight as from 27 April. Hearing of this succession of blows, hands go up to one's head, it is like a nightmare. There is a confusion of languages in my room. I listen to broadcasts in English, Dutch, French and Italian. I listen to everything and you would laugh to see me sitting on my bed totally absorbed, far removed from my own existence. When the announcer says, 'This is England,' my heart starts to race and I greet you my youngest child. Then there is, 'This is the voice of the United States,' and I am with Thys and Hermione; and when it is Sweden, I rejoice with my Goldschmidts. Thank goodness Denmark too can look forward to new life and enjoy its King, and poor Holland need no longer suffer from cruel starvation. If only Ernst and Tilly Sachs have survived all the terror. I have no news of Jacoba and Fritz, and that is dreadful for me, for they of all people were the most faithful and reliable companions throughout the dark years of ever-increasing burdens and privations. What would we have done without Jacoba's *never*-ceasing help and assistance? And no news from Tante Ida in Munich either, very sadly missed. When I think of all our dead : Jasper and Jan in 1942; Roland in 1943; Gustav Heinrich and Mimi in 1944 – all of whom would have made you so very welcome and for whom you will look out in vain, I mourn their departure. God bless them all.

Yesterday W. was elected as Pro-Rector of the University. Behind him there is a phalanx of people on whom he can rely. A new fighting spirit is in him.

17 May, 1945.

Strangely enough the wireless is working, although the current has
been cut off until 7 o'clock this evening. It seems to be a Polish or
Russian station and I hope it is not saying anything nasty for I
cannot understand a word. Maybe there will soon be a language I
know. Again rumours are circulating about disagreements between
the Soviets and the Anglo-Americans. Thank God all black-out
restrictions have been abolished, because these gave rise to sombre
predictions and rumours. It is as if humanity cannot exist without
some kind of agitation and unfounded foreboding. The Russians
are supposed to have resumed bombing, and to want possession of
Hamburg and Kiel. People here are already scraping and bowing
to the English, trying to find favour. I do understand that W. is
deeply depressed, has little hope for his own particular world. He
was so passionately devoted to Great Britain and all it stood for.
Now he is disillusioned by the limitless arrogance and the dis-
honesty with which they treat us, proclaiming to the whole world
that only Germany could have sunk so low in such abysmal cruelty
and bestiality, that they themselves are pure and beyond reproach.
And *who* destroyed our beautiful cities, regardless of human life,
of women, children or old people? *Who* poured down poisonous
phosphorus during the terror raids on unfortunate fugitives, driving them like living torches into the rivers? *Who* dive-bombed
harmless peasants, women and children, in low-level attacks, and
machine-gunned the defenceless population? *Who* was it, I ask
you? We are all the same, all equally guilty, and if my entire being
was not straining towards a reunion with you, life would be nothing but torture and abhorrence.

New rules and regulations are issued by the Military Government
each evening. We are now allowed to be out till 9 p.m. There is an
obvious and frightening food crisis. We have not had fresh vegetables for days and our meals are a problem. Maria's mood is
predictably awful. We are longing for a good square meal. W. has
been given a large packet of glucose and I am afraid we are all
digging into it, eating it in large spoonfuls. Again, compared with
others, we have been and are incredibly lucky. Despite the countless raids on Hamburg during all those years we had only two
small fires in our flat and nothing drastic happened. We survived
all the attacks and so did our furniture and other belongings, which
we naïvely left to their fate on the third floor. No book is missing

and apart from a few of W.'s shirts, we have lost nothing. Really and truly we should have our own little private thanksgiving service. Did not the ever merciful hand of God shelter and guard us again and again? And did we deserve it? No, we must never forget this, and it must become the basis for a new, hopeful, forward-looking frame of mind. Of course the after-effects of perennial over-excitement, of privation, of undernourishment, cause depression and despondency. No wonder. But avanti!

21 May, 1945. Whit Monday.

The Military Government has decreed that this is *not* a public holiday in Hamburg; everyone is to pursue his occupation. On top of that we have been ordered to remove the huge mountains of refuse from all the street corners, all available manpower has to help. Great consternation and disgust in our house, but all the men, young and old, have shouldered their spades and gone, including W. An area has been cleared for the disposal of rubbish. We can no longer use our large dustbins, but have to carry small buckets direct from the kitchen to this space, which is some distance away. It really is a blessing that those stinking heaps of muck are being dealt with. On the whole things are a bit triste, the question of nourishment a growing problem. Rations have been cut by a third. There are no potatoes at all. We are lucky because, with our own personal strict rationing system, we hoarded some old ones, but the question of fuel is going to be acute again. I am strongly under the impression that our flat, together with all the furniture and all our clothes, needs a good clean and renovation. But there is neither polish nor soap and slowly but surely things deteriorate. I haven't got a single decent tea-cloth, for instance, only tattered bits of rag. It cannot be helped.

There is a lot of incitement and adverse propaganda between the Russians and the Anglo-Americans and what it will lead to, nobody knows. Bürgermeister Krogmann has been arrested and Rudolf Petersen has taken his place. W., as Pro-Rector, has taken over the University administration; Herr Keser was dismissed because he belonged to the previous government. In this circle too there are two factions and all sorts of intrigues. W. was on the point of resignation to begin with, wanted to withdraw from everything in disgust and disappointment. But the men behind him, especially Professor Kroetz, in the end persuaded him to recognize the importance of his post and of his work. We are very friendly with the Kroetz couple. He is the director of the Altona Hospital, and as far as I am concerned an ideal doctor. He is a big strong man with a young, broad and healthy face and possesses a deep fund of warmth and kindness and understanding. He is incredibly kind to us, never visits without some thoughtful present for W., a cigar or a bottle of wine, and his medical care is touching. Frau Kroetz is also a doctor, a full Professor of Medicine, with the reputation of being an important research worker. [Ruth's godfather] Professor Bethe knows her well as she used to work with him in Frankfurt. On first acquaintance she appears a trifle withdrawn and inaccessible, but wins tremendously when one knows her more intimately. They are very different and I am quite fascinated by them both, should like to know what brought them together. They have no children. They came for tea yesterday. It was a gorgeous, sun-drenched Whit Sunday. Maria had managed to produce a very decent cake, made from flour, milk, sugar, a tiny spot of butter and egg powder I believe. They were both of the opinion that Hitler was still alive and hiding somewhere. Himmler has not been arrested yet either; most of the others are behind bars.

27 May, 1945.
Now they have caught Himmler. He was wearing a black patch over one eye in order not to be recognized and actually managed to hide for almost a month. When they caught up with him, he swallowed a capsule of cyanide and was dead within fifteen minutes. In order to perpetuate his rare and aristocratic physiognomy, a death-mask was made.

All we ever hear on the wireless, all the news items in the shoddy little free newspaper we get concern the brutalities of the concentration camps, with lurid pictures and ghastly details. W. is sad and angry, because our enemies accuse *all* of us, without exception, of being criminals, fully responsible for what has happened.

I was interrupted by a visit from Fräulein Blohm, sister of Gesa Blohm, the gymnastics teacher in Neustadt. I was very eager to meet her and to receive the wonderful news that Jacoba will be with us tomorrow. Oh how glad I am, how glad! Herr Blohm is

going to Neustadt by car and will give Jacoba a lift back. At last I
shall hear how they have fared during the past few weeks since we
separated. It has not been quiet in Neustadt, the hospital being
crowded out with patients and doctors, and food supplies inadequate. Fräulein Blohm told me that her sister had only four slices
of bread and a plateful of soup per day. Jacoba must tell me all
about it, and I will try to scrounge a few things for her. I do hope
she and Fritz did not go hungry. What a blessing to see her and
talk to her again! The sun is a little reluctant today, only blinking
now and again through my curtainless windows, which do need the
strong hand of a window cleaner. For days I have been darning
the net-curtains, but they tear like tissue-paper.

If only W. were not quite so depressed. Quite systematically he
is strangling the love for England in his heart, and will not admit,
even to himself, that what he cherished is imperishable and eternal
and has nothing to do with present circumstances. Looking at it
realistically, I cannot quite see how England could react in any
other way. It is not possible to make distinctions between people
and there is indeed sufficient reason to mistrust all of us, as the
other nations do, since Germany tolerated Hitler, their most bitter
and most hated enemy. Ultimately I am sure we can work together;
but meanwhile we will have to bear the yoke, will have to be small
and insignificant and to obey orders. There is no comfort in this,
but it is the truth.

I was going to send in our names for the public soup kitchen, for
we have run out of fuel and I wish the gas would come back.
Yesterday we suddenly had hot water. The English Captain downstairs wants a hot bath every Saturday and has ordered coal for
this purpose. There is general praise for the billeted troops, while
the stories about the Russians in Berlin sound gruesome. But what
credit can one give to gossip after our experiences of the past years?
Some of the people in our house are very odd. Elderly ladies be-
moan the fact that we no longer congregate in the cellar, and miss
the siren at breakfast time! We got to know each other in the
cellar, inevitably formed superficial relationships through shared
anxieties, and a cosy system of gossip grew up. As in politics, the
most far-fetched rumours float through our old house. We still see
a good bit of the Leiser family, partly because of my great fondness
for their small daughter, and hers for me. Apart from that we live
even more quietly than before, are still not allowed out after 9

p.m. and have very little public transport. We did manage to see our friends the von Gosslers briefly the other day, and today we are actually expecting the Schlensogs here. He has returned unharmed and without difficulties. So many are still missing. Tante Irmgard knows nothing of her husband or son. The husbands of your cousins Renate and Eva are probably prisoners of war. Your other cousin Esther Sommer had a marvellous surprise when her youngest son Ehrhard, a pupil in one of the Hitler schools, suddenly appeared, having walked all the way, three weeks, from Sonthofen. My masseuse, nice Frau Sprenger, has had no news at all from her son and daughter-in-law. She had tea with me yesterday and complained bitterly about the reallocation of hospitals. The patients and staff of the large Barmbeck Hospital have been moved, lock, stock and barrel to a much smaller, older one in Wandsbeck, while the original is used as a field-hospital for troops. A lot of the doctors are particularly hard hit since they have had to move out of their official residences.

1 June, 1945.
Soon it will be the longest day. But one cannot really make the most of these nice long evenings, the general mood being one of depression. Mistakenly it was assumed that everything would be better and easier once the war was over, and now it is almost as if the very opposite had happened. Daily life is fraught with small and very small difficulties, and the really major ones are almost overlooked. The main reason is tiredness; it is more obvious now what havoc the past years have played with people, how they have just given up. Standing in queues from morning till night for a tiny cabbage or lettuce; the uncertainty of cooking facilities, of finding fuel, since there is no gas and electricity is rationed; the huge question 'What shall we eat?'; the other, equally important question 'How shall we wash our dirty linen?'; after carting loads to the laundry and receiving them back by no means cleaner, unironed and with no starch – all this does not make for cheerful days. Added to this is the complete absence of mail for over a month now, and a flood of new regulations from the Military Government. W. has gone from one extreme to the other, is indignant and furious about everything England does, thinks they are all hypocrites, and self-righteous puritans, but I really cannot see how they

could behave in any other way at present. After all, we are the vanquished and deserve to be despised together with all those scoundrels who drove us to subservience and perdition. We are reminded daily on the radio and in the pathetic little newssheet of our responsibility for the unspeakable horrors that were perpetrated in the concentration camps, and it serves us right. Nobody can escape this collective guilt.

We had a lot of detailed news from Jacoba. To my intense delight she came last Monday at 8 o'clock in the morning with a Red Cross car. They were trying to get a replacement issue of drugs for her hospital. And as always she brought us wonderful things : butter, cheese, sausage, jam and coffee – bless her. I cannot tell you how good it was to have her back. Separation from her was more difficult to bear than from any of you during those long years. We have been through so much together, side by side, bonded by indestructible ties. What she told us about the last days of the war in Neustadt was almost unbelievable. Prior to the final arrival of the British garrison along the entire coast – which took place at the same time as ours – Neustadt bay had one dive-bomb attack after another, because a number of big German boats had taken refuge there, including the *Cap Arcona* with 13,000 concentration camp evacuees from East Prussia. The British air force, not knowing that, thought they were ordinary fugitives and dropped so many bombs on the boat that it burst into flames and sank. Thousands were drowned, but many swam ashore in a state of complete exhaustion, verminous, and had to be admitted to the hospital. Other patients had to give up their beds, were accommodated on the floor on straw palliasses and the concentration camp victims were made comfortable. They had the best food which could be provided, and the others had to go hungry, had only a cup of thin ersatz-coffee and one piece of bread in the morning, a plateful of soup thickened with bruised grain and a piece of bread for lunch, more coffee and another piece of bread in the evening. Jacoba's T.B. patients went into a decline, while the concentration camp patients were quite unable to digest the unaccustomed food, contracted dysentery and got worse. In their concentration camp they had slept sixteen women to one wooden plank and had long since given up even the most primitive forms of behaviour. They did everything on the floor, hardly getting out of bed. Lice were running across their faces and all the staff and

11 Tilli Wolff-Mönckeberg, c. 1954.

12 Emil Wolff, Tilli, Jacoba and Fritz Hahn in April 1946.

13 Andreasstrasse 39. The Wolffs' flat was on the third floor.

14 Andreasstrasse today.

doctors' wives had to set to to delouse them. They now have an epidemic of spotted typhus.

Needless to say I am anxious about Jacoba and Fritz. Fritz-chen's hylus gland infection had to be punctured. He is much better, plays wild games with two boys of his own age, but he has not recovered completely. A sixteen-year-old schoolboy is giving the three of them some lessons; thank goodness he is starting to learn again! Jacoba has had to move out of one of her rooms, for every inch of accommodation is needed, even the bathrooms. Although she is working without respite all day long and Sundays as well, she gives the impression of being more cheerful, firmer in herself and not a bit down-hearted, a blessing for us as usual. With courage and energy she has reorganized the distribution of food supplies to patients and staff and has managed to achieve various additions to the rations. Fritz's ward-sister sees to it that he gets all the extras he is entitled to, and Jacoba always seems to have some-thing to spare even for us. They had only four nurses per 200 patients, and the doctors had to give a hand everywhere. There is still no certainty that the Hospital Superintendent will remain in office. Everybody who belonged to the Nazi Party prior to 1933 will be dismissed. Dr Cornits has always been very decent to Jacoba, esteems her as a colleague and a human being.

Jacoba told me a story which she had heard from a refugee from Elbing. This person was alone in her home with three small children. Her husband was a soldier. Three Russian officers came to her door and asked politely whether she had any alcoholic spirits for them. Then they told her that she had the choice between sexual intercourse with all three of them or death. Not wanting to desert her children, she submitted. This is not an isolated case.

2 June, 1945.

I have had a long afternoon rest and a strong cup of real tea, which revived me. I was absolutely worn out after hanging around the food office all morning, where we had to hand over certain items of clothing for the foreign labour force. A complete suit for a man, plus shirt, collar and tie, pants, two pairs of socks, two hand-kerchiefs and a pillowcase; a frock, a blouse and a handkerchief for a woman. Why not collect these things for our own bombed-out compatriots or the concentration camp victims? What concern of

E

ours are the foreign workers, who stand around and do not seem
to do anything at all? There were many disparaging remarks in my
queue. I squatted steadfastly on my suitcase and sent W. home.
Afterwards I went to fetch twelve pounds of rhubarb from my
hairdresser and arrived home with back-ache. But the cups of tea
have done wonders and now I am thinking of you with a lot more
intensity. I have been re-reading my diaries of the year 1938, the
year of my kidney operation, and still feel so richly rewarded by
all your love and attention. How poverty-stricken I am now with
only memories to warm me! And where are you all? Jella and
Hellmuth with all their children had to flee to Stockholm to escape
the fiendish persecution of the Jews in Denmark; Dr Jacoba and
Fritz are in Neustadt, her husband dead; Jan is dead; Thys and
Hermione and two children have been in Chicago for the past
seven years; Ruth and Ifor are in Wales with their two little ones.
The stream of love which then flowed to me without hindrance,
now has to force its way over vast distances, perhaps unable to find
me, for you do not even know whether I am still alive. In 1938
three dear daughters came to see me on my birthday, and how you
all spoilt me! All I can do today is to thank you once again for
making me so rich and happy. Think of me quietly and peacefully,
even if you should not see me again. One day perhaps these pages
will land in your hands, a testimony of the most terrible time
Germany ever experienced, the most bitter period we were forced
to witness. We are poor, downtrodden and despised by all.

12 June, 1945.
Since I wrote to you last, my dear ones, many things have changed
again. Yes, the first little tiny threads have been spun to connect
us again, and I even had a chance to write the first uncensored
words to you, although I do not know whether these tentative little
feelers will reach you. But the very fact of sensing a possibility
that words from me might get to you has given me immeasurable
joy.

The other evening, it was Saturday in fact, our doorbell rang
loudly and W. went downstairs to open the door to an English
officer with a rifle over his shoulder. W. thought he had come to
arrest him. But no, the officer said at once that his home was in
Aberystwyth! In next to no time he was upstairs with us, sitting

in W.'s big armchair and reading us a paragraph from his father's letter. His name was Evans, too, and Ifor knows his father. The letter said that the Principal's wife was desperately anxious to have some news of her family and was very worried about everybody. It also said that she and the children were very well. I was so excited and moved that only bits of broken English came tumbling out, but W. immediately wrote down a message which the officer was going to add to a letter to his father that very evening. We were not permitted to write ourselves because of the strict censorship. In the end we drank a bottle of wine together, he gave us some very good cigarettes and it was as if we were old friends. He is a very nice man, not all that young any more, by profession an engineer and as opposed to war as we are. He looked so healthy, a full face with big cheeks, tanned by the sun, thick, dark hair and sparkling white, strong teeth. He stayed with us until 10 o'clock and we forgot all about supper. He will come again as soon as he has had a reply from his father, and he also said he would bring us 'some food', which would be lovely. Perhaps by now, my darling Ruth, you will have already got this reassuring message from us. Jella too might have received my tentative message. Frau Zassenhaus rang me up to say that she knew of a very reliable Norwegian officer who would send on letters from Denmark to Stockholm, and of course I wrote at once.

Our town has changed its face again. The original garrison has left, but whether this second one is the last we do not yet know. The billets in our house have been vacated, the army vehicles have left the road, and it all looks quite normal again. The regulations remain the same, strictly no one in the road after 10.15 p.m. and curfew at 9 p.m. etc. General Montgomery's speech has produced considerable indignation, and I cannot understand what he hoped to gain by it.* The English soldiers were particularly friendly with our children, and nobody complained about discourtesy and unpleasantness; on the contrary, they gave away chocolates and the children thought it was wonderful to watch them in their comings and goings and their large cars.

*On 10 June, 1945 Montgomery made a broadcast on Hamburg radio explaining that British troops had been ordered not to fraternize with the German population. His aim in ordering non-fraternization was that 'this time', as opposed to 1918, 'you should learn your lesson: not only that you have been defeated . . . but that you – your nation – were guilty of beginning a war.'

We have now decided, since Jacoba drew my attention to enormous cobwebs in the corner of my room, to do some spring-cleaning after all, even if we have not got the necessary where-withal, like soap and polish. The somewhat dim charwoman of our neighbours, who have left for good, comes to us every day and delightedly shares our food. She is a touching little creature, terribly poor, but of a happy disposition. She always hums little ditties when she stands on the ladder in her outsize felt slippers. Whether she is truly thorough, I rather doubt, but at least every bit of furniture is moved and the walls are dusted down. Redecoration is out of the question. Life is still very fatiguing, especially the queueing for vegetables. We have worked out a routine, the three of us take it in turns and with our small camp-stool we can at least sit down. Most women take their breakfast along and darn stock-ings while they wait outside the shops from 9 o'clock in the morn-ing until at least 3 o'clock. The lorries do not arrive until 2. What is torture for us, some of them regard as entertainment. Quite frequently they quarrel, become downright abusive and all but hit each other.

As Rector, officially confirmed by Bürgermeister Petersen, W. has a great deal to do and is beleaguered from all sides. I am glad for him, for although he looks very delicate, psychologically speak-ing it was the best that could happen to him. He can use his tremendous intellectual acumen and all his diplomatic ability to best advantage, can truly 'reign' like a monarch. He had an audience with the Bürgermeister and yesterday with Major Shelton of the British Control Commission. Both meetings were satisfactory as far as he was concerned. He was at once handed a long-term permit for direct access to the local administration, and has managed to start proceedings for the return of the books which were sent away from all the libraries. There is still no post, and we continue to break up our chairs to heat our kitchen range. Thus time passes; soon we will have the longest day, Fritzchen's tenth birthday and Thys's wedding anniversary. Our nights are quiet and we can sleep, and the radio no longer screams at us, 'Attention, attention, enemy fighter planes are approaching our frontiers.' Instead it is, 'This is England, you are listening to a report from the United Nations,' or 'These are the regulations of the Military Government.' One takes it all in one's stride, ceases to be surprised. Have we really run as dry as that? I cannot understand mankind.

The greatest nastiness and the greatest stupidity are swallowed down with the same kind of indifference. Good night, my treasures! —

17 June, 1945.
I wonder if Jacoba and Fritz will come today? I woke up very early full of restlessness and anticipation. A gentleman called yesterday. His son is in the Neustadt hospital and he can go by car there and back. He brought me a letter from Jacoba. She has been very poorly but thank goodness is better now and her temperature is normal, only she is still very weak and limp, and I wish she would come here so that I could nurse and look after her. She does not know yet whether there will be transport. Here I am ready and waiting, arms and heart wide open for her.

We continue to spring-clean and have reached Tante Lulu's room. W.'s den and his library were a trial. For hours I stood on the stepladder, trying to clean the books. Showers of flaky dirt and dust confronted me. Maria has washed all the windows and window-sills and Frau Tiedgen muddled around happily. It is a nice feeling that the dirt of the war years has been brushed out. I wish one could spring-clean one's soul too. Beastly things still happen daily. What one hears about the Russians is disgusting. You wonder if it is true. The Russians are keen to have as many children as possible in Germany. Women have to work during the day, then to make themselves attractive at night, ready to receive and please the Russian gentlemen! In Berlin husbands have to leave their homes in the evening, the front-doors must be open, and their wives and daughters at the disposal of the conquerors. General Eisenhower stated publicly that the Russian people are the kindest in the world. Prisoners of war from other countries are flooding back to their homelands. German soldiers are released to do agricultural work, have to see to it that we have enough to eat. Prospects for the winter are very poor. For the time being we get by and manage to acquire some vegetables by patient queueing. But this crouching around on camp-stools is an absurd waste of time and energy and the women with whom one sits and waits and gets into inevitable contact with are not exactly congenial. 'Look at that old granny,' one said to me the other day, 'she's half decomposed already, you can smell it.' And then they start on

'that cur, that swine, that Hitler', the man they could not praise
highly enough only a little while ago! Ribbentrop too has been
found at last, here in Hamburg. He was living with his girl-friend
in a very second-rate boarding house. What a choice lot they are!

I am sorry to say it is cold and grey and not like summer.
Yesterday we had hot water, and we bathed and washed our
clothes like mad. I was in bed by 9.30. In the afternoon Tante
Lulu and I had a very comfortable little tea together in my room.
I had brewed some strong real tea and we had a piece of home-
made currant bread. We read choice episodes from Goethe's
Dichtung und Wahrheit, and finally listened to a Goethe song
cycle on the radio, *An die ferne Geliebte.* We were very conscious
of our good fortune compared with many others. Only spontaneous
gaiety is missing, because you are missing. The relationship between
my dear sister and me is sometimes a little strained. I feel that all
my life I have had to fight this hopeless battle with my impatient
and intolerant self and I never win. I flatter myself that I should
be better able to sustain large demands on my endurance. Coping
with the continuous small, everyday tasks constitutes after all the
most important part of human education, and is, perhaps, the most
difficult to learn. Today is Sunday and peace. Amongst us too!
Maria, in mellow mood, has even brought W. a cup of real coffee
from her ration.

25 June, 1945.
Jacoba and Fritz alas never came, and I have had no news from
them since they announced their visit. I am worried about Jacoba
because she is ill. I have heard that there were 1,200 cases of
spotted typhus in Germany. I wrote her a postcard but have had
no reply. It is now possible to send a 6-pfennig card with the code
No. 24; you hand it in unfranked at the post office and it will make
its way slowly towards its destination. The inspiring motto and the
Hitler profile have been cut off. I do hope my two in Neustadt are
well. There is no news from Thys or Jella either. Jella's last letter
was dated 18 March, 1945. But there are several messages from
Ruth from various directions, and yesterday a letter from Ifor to
W. via Major Shelton. What joy! They are all well and Ruth was
beside herself with delight on receiving our message, she also knows
that W. has been elected Rector. They seem to have known this

for some time. Now I feel, just one more step and we shall be together again. I have written to her three times during the past weeks. Once Jacoba thought a British parachutist would take the letter; once Frau Zassenhaus hoped the Norwegian officer might post one; and the third I gave to Schlinck. Jella too should have had a long letter. If only all these signs of life and love have reached them!

W. is terribly busy. Consultations in the mornings, committees and meetings in the afternoons, and people, people all the time wanting his advice. He looks tired, but his mind is as active as ever, and I am sure he is in the right place. Every day there is renewed happiness in me because I know what it means to him, and what he means to others. I asked him to have coffee with me this afternoon. I enjoy my own room during the summer. It is so bright and light, my very own small kingdom with my pictures and books, my desk and Ruth's doll. We sat together so harmoniously, sipping coffee, he smoking and I darning and writing. Funnily enough it felt almost like being on holiday, released from household duties. Coffee stimulates my imagination and my emotions. Our friendship with Herr and Frau Kroetz is growing daily and I am very pleased about it. On Saturdays, when W. has a seminar, Frau Kroetz and I meet to read English together. The first time we just chatted and did not read a word. She is a very remarkable academic, renowned throughout her profession, has published many important pieces of research, and with all this a most likable woman, quite unpretentious and not a bit intellectually overbearing. I am proud that she trusts me. This is the kind of relationship I value, an unconventional get-together, without constraint, straightforward and cordial. We meet nearly every day. So many people these days are bowed down by some excruciating fate. I shall have to tell you about it another time.

30 June, 1945.
My darling Jella, it is your 42nd birthday, and for the first time in your life there is no loving message from me. But you must know that I am thinking of you every hour of the day with fondness and gratitude, that I wish for you and all your family only the very best. The day before yesterday I heard from Jacoba – a letter brought by hand by a chemist who was in Hamburg to get new

drug supplies – that your friend Lars Gravesen had been to see her, and to her intense delight brought loving messages from you. What a small world it is after all! I have had five different messages from Ruth already and was able to reply through the kindness of others. I do hope I shall soon hear from you too, my dearest Goldschmidts. We also heard from Ifor that they had made contact with Tilly and Ernst Sachs in Holland. Thank God they are alive and well after the terrible experience of occupation and starvation.

I wonder how and where you are celebrating your birthday. I am sure the children will have lots of surprises for you. If only we can celebrate together again next year! 'That depends on Churchill and on God,' a nice elderly British naval officer said to me the other day when he visited us and I told him one or two things about us. I felt like talking, my English better than usual. I told him that the English people were mistaken in their opinion that *all* Germans were Nazis, that we were *all* collectively responsible for our present dilemma and had to do penance for the Nazi Government. I tried to explain our own personal opinion. We hated the régime from the very beginning, abhorred it more day by day. But it was totally impossible to form an opposition, spied upon as we were from all sides, telephone conversations listened in to, people standing behind us and alongside us listening and denouncing. It would have cost us our lives, or we should have ended up in concentration camps. All through those years we stood by our Jewish friends, never made a secret of it; W. continued to give lectures on England and never said anything which he could not back honestly with a clear and unsullied conscience. We could do no more. Personally I have never given the Hitler salute and when I was supposed to I murmured something else instead. I think we would have been prepared to commit murder to get rid of that scoundrel. The past six years were a period of unadulterated suffering and torture and increasing slavery. And now our ardently longed-for deliverance means only that we are despised and hated, objects of contempt, and have to face further starvation. Alright, we have to go on hoping, bearing our cross meanwhile. If I tell you of some of the unspeakable conditions many people have to put up with – and I will do so, perhaps tomorrow – you will say that your mother is exaggerating and imagining things. I can only repeat that we personally must have had a guardian angel watching over us.

1 July, 1945.

I remember that in the spring of 1939, when I returned from England, I went to visit Walter Goldschmidt in Antwerp, and met my dear niece Tilly [Sachs-Sieveking, Tante Lulu's daughter]. We tramped through the town together and had so much to tell each other that once or twice we were nearly run over. In the cathedral, right in front of the large crucifixion by Rubens, Tilly said, almost screaming and with flaming eyes, 'If I had a large kitchen-knife, I would thrust it into that criminal Hitler.' Imagine the semi-darkness of that big church, the mighty black cross on the painting, heavy and menacing against a blood-red sunset, and us two women filled with bloodthirsty thoughts.

But also imagine this. A young woman, seven months pregnant, had to flee with her two small boys from the Russians in Mecklenburg. One of the boys had been operated on for appendicitis only two days previously, the other one had dysentery. The only vehicle available was a farm-cart on which she piled some belongings and off she went. She harnessed the old horse, drove it herself, cooked meals en route, and after a fortnight arrived eventually at her father's house here in Hamburg. We know him by name; her brother-in-law, her sister's husband, is a colleague of W.'s. Vilma and Kollmar also fled from the Russians in three stages and have now arrived in Hamburg. When I heard Vilma's voice over the phone, I thought it came from a world beyond. We had given up hope of ever seeing them again, since we knew that the Russians had landed in the Lausitz. One day, I hope, she will tell me in peace and quiet about their escape. When they came to tea the other day we were all far too excited. Waves of happiness at our reunion swept over us, mixed with the after-pains of all our bereavements and grief. Everybody talked at once, each eager to impart what seemed most important. They have been able to salvage hardly anything, and had to leave their exquisite home, with all its art treasures, books and memories, in the rapacious hands of the Russians. At the very last moment, at the dead of night and in complete darkness, they got onto a lorry with Marlene and her friend, and set off. They were able to drive through the Russian lines, which had already moved beyond them, because the soldiers on guard were too busy canoodling with Ukrainian women to be interested in them. In Meissen, the Russians caught up with them again and on went the flight. The most difficult part was crossing the Elbe. Kollmar looks like an old man. Vilma will win through. She immediately managed to obtain an immigration permit into our zone and Bürgermeister Petersen has granted her indefinite asylum.

6 July, 1945.
Tired, tired. If anything, this summer is even more difficult than the last. We are very short of food and one's entire interest is concentrated in this direction. It is the absence of fat which makes one so greedy. I have fantastic visions of sausages, beefsteaks, luscious cakes with whipped cream, large bowls of fruit, platters of mixed vegetables – young peas, beans, red tomatoes, pale green cucumbers, tender cauliflower and provocative asparagus with butter, a dance of inviting and alluring things before my mind's eye. At the best delicatessen shop in town you get a bit of mince and dehydrated vegetables that taste like straw, no potatoes, and at best an indefinable brew of soup. If only one could exist without food! I am going to bed, it is cold and grey, not a pleasant summer evening. Irmgard Lieven, Gisela Markert's sister, and her eight-month-old baby are staying with us.

8 July, 1945.
Today there is a little sunshine, my dear, far-away children. I have asked W. to have coffee with me again and have even made two pieces of toast from our bread ration. We have crept away into our room, for the flat is much too full, we old hermits are not used to that.

The understanding, generous, unconventional part of me is fighting a losing battle with the pernickety, obstinate and exacting Hamburg lady, who hates the untidy bathroom with its everlasting pile of smelly, dirty nappies, constant splashes, wet floors and the unclean use of my special basin, cigarette ash in inappropriate places, chaos in the kitchen and never a clean saucepan, cup or spoon. Good old Irmgard has led a sort of gypsy existence for years, is by nature untidy and slapdash, even with her baby, and does not conform to my views on child care, which you have learned from me. Little Andreas is such an easy baby, always contented and happy. He only gets angry when he is hungry and she takes very little notice, very often not giving him his last feed until 9 o'clock at night, poor little thing. He sleeps in the cot which was bought once upon a time in Amsterdam for Henkie. It then had delicate, soft organdie drapes and yellow silk ribbons, also the finest bedlinen your father could buy. A year later he died in that same small cot on a glowing Italian summer evening. You have all slept in it, one after the other, and subsequently Jella's children, except Michael. I adore this little cot. You can tell it has had some buffeting. During the war I lent it to various people, and in our air-raid shelter it harboured many an exhausted child. Now little Andreas crawls about in it, a friendly, fatherless small boy, reminding me a bit of Thys with his fair hair and blue eyes. I am glad I decided to take these two homeless little people in, and now, having confessed my weakness, I realize the pettiness of it all and will not let it consume me.

I had faithful Senkpiel to help me empty Mimi's room and I am quite proud that I managed it. Maria was away staying with her sister in Pinneberg, so I had to clean and tidy the room, dismember the cobwebs and brush out little piles of dirt. It looks nice and friendly now. Strange to relate, Maria has taken very kindly to the increase in our family, looks upon the child with warm, motherly eyes and even tolerates the invasion of her kitchen. She was unable to bring anything back from Pinneberg. There are plenty of vegetables and fruit there, but most of it is immediately commandeered by the British Army, which the farmers deplore. And it is rather shocking; after all they have an abundance of food and we, poor devils, have nothing. The few items she had scrounged for us had to be left behind, because the lorry which gave her a lift was too full. They were stowed in like cattle, standing-room only, swaying round the corners and almost precipitated into the road. The old dear came home with the words, 'I'm nothing but a living corpse,' covered with bruises all over her body and squashed toes – but, alas, no peas and beans.

All this shoving and pushing is, I am afraid, typical of the general attitude, as if people have to let out their fury on others. It is virtually impossible to get concert tickets for instance. The booking-office opens at 10 a.m. and crowds begin to form outside at 7 a.m. As soon as the queue starts to move, pressure from the back lifts the people in front off their feet and they can barely save themselves. Hats and handbags are squashed and torn off, elbowing and kicking follows, accompanied by fitting curses. We don't even try any more, would rather forgo the pleasure of live music and listen to the concerts on the radio. Just now there was a broadcast of a Beethoven largo for flute and piano, serene and beautiful. The first couple of symphony concerts were of course an occasion in Hamburg, as was the huge circus and fairground on the Moor-weide, with a big tent for the performances, caravans, slides and merry-go-rounds. Crowds of little children flattened their noses against the outside fence, but they were not allowed in. There was one performance for the local children the other day, but the police marched in and ordered them out, and lo and behold the British personnel also left in protest. I liked that.

We do not see very much of the Tommies in our district, but meet them in other places, looking healthy, sun-tanned and strong, rifles over their shoulders, and we see their cars and large motor vehicles. Traffic in Hamburg has resumed its bustle and speed, which is odd after the drab silence of the war years. I hardly ever go into town, but W. goes every day, sometimes twice. Contrary to his usual habits, he has to leave the house very early and sits in his official consulting-room at the Bornplatz every morning. He comes home for lunch, pale and fatigued, and we are in a dither until he arrives, trying to keep his food hot, because we are so short of fuel. Maria grumbles and our stomachs complain noisily. Three days a week we have no electricity from 7 a.m. onwards and there is no other means of cooking, except the electric kettle and a highly-treasured hot-plate. So Mother gets up at 6 o'clock and makes tea or coffee before 7, while the others sleep. It is not at all like summer, rather grey and unpleasant, except for the real joy when we are with the Kroetzes. Their lovely home at the Harvestehuder-weg has been badly damaged, yet what is left is most comfortable and tasteful. Once a week we have dinner with them, all four of us happy in each other's company, quite apart from their generous hospitality. There is also joy in W.'s success as Rector. It spurs him on, he is lively and animated, and he has a good relationship with the British administration. Slowly but surely he is regaining his confidence in England. He had a long conversation with an English artist the other day and was full of enthusiasm. Those that are cultured and educated still maintain a very high level of intelligence.

What else brings me happiness? Certainly the rare letters from Jacoba which float into my hands, when a patient of hers comes from Neustadt, or the chemist, who buys drugs and brings a much longed-for letter as well as a lovely parcel from your sister. She always thinks of us, is concerned 'that you won't shrivel up, get smaller and thinner'. She is back at work after a bout of spotted typhus. Thank heaven it was only a mild attack. Fritzchen's condition is satisfactory too, but he still has to rest every day, has to be very careful, and this worries me. I often long for a few quiet days in Neustadt, for Jacoba's selfless care, her warmth and concern. Frequently in the mornings I wish I could sit down to a proper breakfast, ready and prepared. But, dear Tilli, do not forget how much better off you are than the majority of people. Do remember it!

Tante Lili [Siemsen, her cousin] was evicted from her house in the Badestrasse and has to be content with one room in her mother's old house. And she was always so spoilt and particular. Today this place was like an hotel, with so many telephone calls and discussions, and now, at 9 o'clock in the evening, Herr Leiser is here to consult with W. about important business concerning this house. That is the end of a quiet Sunday. I have just thought of another joy of my life. Goethe's *West-Östliche Divan*. The more I get to know it, the more I am able to absorb and comprehend its beauty. How good the aphorisms are, how splendid the individual books of this work, always interspersed with verses of extreme simplicity and beauty. I am learning several verses by heart so that they can live on inside me. We are not dried up intellectually, on the contrary, I occasionally even feel lively and productive, do not see myself as a tough and stale old piece of cake.

Stories of individual hardships sustained by fugitives should be written down and documented. They are so unbelievable that future generations will doubt their credibility, and they *are* true. Dangers and deprivations have snowballed into such fantastic experiences. We met an acquaintance the other day who had returned from Theresienstadt concentration camp, and she is going to tell us what happened; poor woman, she looks broken and terrible. Where are all the others who were deported? How many will return? How many won't?

Farewell for today with fond thoughts, my dear ones. Are you able to visualize our Hamburg? Two of the five proud spires, St Jacobi and St Katharine, are missing from the skyline, but like a silver mirror the Alster still reflects the green garland of trees, and the Elbe flows serenely and majestically past verdant shores; we love this river, which has so much grace, so much freshness, and reflects so many many ruins. Wherever you look there are small allotments growing vegetables for the hungry, vitamin-deprived inhabitants. In every front garden, in all the empty squares, you find beans instead of roses, potatoes instead of summer flowers. Want stares at you from every countenance, peeps round every corner. Bitterness and anguish have carved harsh lines into every face. Where is hope? Where joy? One still has to be patient, patient, as we have had to be for six long years.

13 July, 1945.

> *Wie? Wann? und Wo? – Die Götter bleiben stumm!*
> *Du halte dich ans Weil, und frage nicht Warum?**
>
> *Prüft das Geschick Dich, weiss es wohl warum:*
> *Es wünschte dich enthaltsam! Folge stumm.*†

Goethe, *Buch der Sprüche, West-Östlicher Divan.*

A letter comes from Jacoba. She writes that there is panic; the Russians are supposed to be taking over Neustadt and the entire Baltic coast. W. thinks that it is only a rumour, like so many many others, so that people will have no chance to settle down. Jacoba also says that all she is longing for are a few peaceful years of uninterrupted work in Neustadt without excitements and upheavals and having to think about escaping; but she does not think her generation will ever achieve a state of peace. Poor darling, she is the quintessence of fortitude and courage. Something else is making me feel very uneasy. Lotte Caspari phoned me the other day, saying that she did not think it beyond the range of possibility that 'the boys', as she called Thys and her brother Fritz, might be called up to fight the Japanese. God forbid! I am full of sad forebodings today. The weather has changed again, it's suddenly cold and

---

*From *Lyrische Dichtungen, Weimar 1810-12* by Goethe. Translation:
  How? When? and Where? – The Gods will not reply!
  Hold fast onto the day, do not ask why.
†Translation (by Alexander Rogers):
  If fate should try thee, wouldst thou know the cause?
  'Twould have thee sober. Follow dumb its laws.

windy after a short spell of heat. We have just listened to a Mozart piano concerto, magic music, which lures out all my longing wistfulness.

18 July, 1945.

Another cold day. When I remember those furnace-like July days forty-three years ago – my God what an age! – I can still feel that glowing heat of an Italian July, smell the heavy perfume of the yellow roses on the terrace. It is forty-three years since you left me, my little eldest son. Perhaps a happy fate removed you so soon from this ugly, nasty world. We liked to let our imagination roam after you left us and fancied we saw you playing on a green meadow with your Dutch grandmother. She chose your name, Hendrik Jolle, and you became the embodiment of everything good and beautiful for her, brought new warmth and light into her life. You fulfilled a remarkable mission in your tiny little life, giving a dying woman comfort and hope when your small hands played with the blanket on her bed. I have suddenly realized that that was the meaning of your being, and when she died, your life's purpose was fulfilled. You went when your task was done, and to ask why was superfluous.

I have not been into town for ages, but I went this morning to deliver a letter for Jacoba at an address at the Alsterdamm. I wandered through the devastated streets as if in a dream. Is your imagination rich enough to picture the power of evil which set in motion this kind of diabolical destruction? I cannot believe it, for even my powers of fantasy can barely reconstruct that reality. I find it hard to revert to those days and nights of heavy terror attacks, the infernal noise of thunder and explosion, the raging rain of fire from the sky, screaming mines, burning incendiaries, death-bringing direct hits, the carpet of bombs over whole streets, and such conflagrations that a sea of cruel light made night into day, throwing into sharp relief crumbling walls, demolished houses, uprooted trees and lamp-posts, craters and corpses on thoroughfares. It is necessary to remember, to realize that we *lived through* and *survived* this. You might think that I am exaggerating, exploiting my fantasy. You will have to come and see for yourself the ruins, remains of buildings, piles of rubble and enormous gaps in the face of our city. Perhaps then you will believe me and shake your head

as I do now, marvelling that it was possible that one did not lose
one's reason. Yes, outwardly all is quiet again, except that in the
centre the bustle and traffic is worse than before. Up go the arms
of the military police to regulate the passage of the innumerable
English vehicles through the streets, and hordes of brown-uni-
formed Tommies are everywhere. They are even allowed to talk to
us outlaws. Yet they eat our vegetables and fruit, and now in
mid-summer we get only sauerkraut and dehydrated food, never
see a cherry or a raspberry. Thus we are made to understand
that we deserve punishment.

At this moment in time, the three illustrious gentlemen, Truman,
Churchill and Stalin, are meeting in Sans Souci to decide our fate.
I wonder what '*der alte Fritz*' [Frederick the Great] would have
had to say about that.

A couple of bowls of thin soup for lunch have not satisfied me,
and now, at 5 o'clock, I cannot make tea because there is no electricity, nor can I afford a piece of bread. I covet something sweet.
Perhaps I had better stop and prepare myself for the English literature and history lessons I have undertaken to give Marlene
[Kollmar] and her friend. I am sitting amongst vast tomes and I
am very keen. Bless you all!

30 July, 1945.
Today is a day of joy. My heart is palpitating, sending warm waves
of happiness racing through my whole being. A long letter has
arrived from my Ruth, such a lovely letter that W. and I could not
restrain our tears. Yes, I can imagine your tortured uncertainty
about us, and we must never forget how mercifully we were
preserved, I can hardly fathom it myself sometimes. Ruth's letter
was handed to W. very surreptitiously during a meeting about the
future of the University.

Now it is nearly August, that sounds a bit like autumn and we
dread the idea of winter with no coal, little to eat and the threat of
general famine. It is a grim thought that there will be months of
frost and cold. We are reminded of our duty to lay in stores of
wood. But where can we get it? There is nothing more to chop up,
our kitchen range has not been lit for days and we have to make do
with the electric kettle and the hot-plate, useless on those days
when there is no current. Maria takes it all as a personal affront.

She went off a week ago with a suitcase full of empty preserving-jars; I hope she will bring them back full. We fetch a daily meal from the British 'cook room' just opposite us, and we are quite happy with it. It is alternately a thin soup, followed by potatoes and gravy, or a thick soup with potatoes in it. It tastes good. The saucepan is put on the table and I deal it out on the plates, potatoes as well. That is the quickest and saves washing up. For supper I invent something, usually just potatoes again, boiled in their skins, accompanied by the boot-polish caviare. Occasionally we have buttermilk and a little sugar, or I serve a sort of custard with fruit juice. Bread is in very short supply, but the white bread is really snowy white, made from English wheatflour, the rolls too. It is quite disgusting that food should play such a major role in our lives, or rather the absence of craved-for items of food. I dream of cream cakes, filled chocolates and whipped cream, and it makes me quite ill to think of them. But please don't think that my mind is entirely possessed by material things. No, I have started teaching, trying to introduce Marlene Kollmar and her friend Karin to English history and literature, quite a bold undertaking. I started right at the very beginning with England's earliest inhabitants, the Celts, and alongside the historical development, I intend to give an outline of contemporary literature. We have now reached Chaucer. I was scared at first, but we are making progress and the girls are very keen and enthusiastic, which makes it much easier. I feel quite elated and content after each lesson, and my inferiority complexes are pushed firmly into a corner.

I am waiting for news from Jacoba today and hope that she and Fritz will be here soon. My evacuee is leaving on 1 August. Little Andreas has been put into a children's home. I will not weep many tears when the mother goes, for she has got on my nerves very badly with her harsh, loud, rapid talk, her untidiness and her squalor. Admittedly everybody is exceptionally touchy, which does not help communication. The best evenings are still the ones with Professor and Frau Kroetz. We have become very firm friends. Now I must prepare myself for tomorrow's lesson, the fat books are waiting for me. Incidentally the University will be re-opened on 16 August! My 'Magnificence', the Rector, has an awful lot to do, and I am sure he is doing it exceptionally well. Bless him.

14 August, 1945.

Rain, rain, nothing but rain. What a summer! The leaves are
changing colour, brown and yellow, and are falling on the wet,
slippery roads. The girls did not turn up for their lesson, and I was
ready to tell them about Langland, Gower and Wycliffe. Marlene
telephoned to say with much regret that she has only one pair of
shoes, the rain would ruin them, and she could not come barefoot.
So please would I not be angry. I decided to indulge in a quiet
afternoon, tidy my books and lie on the sofa reading. But it was not
to be. The telephone rang incessantly for me and for W. and the
doorbell too. Maria was out, queueing for fish. She returned unexpectedly yesterday and I was not overjoyed. It had been so
peaceful without her and I was quite happy to be sole ruler of my
little home. But at once I was forced to recognize her great good
qualities. She has filled thirty preserving-jars for us, and when she
goes back to Pinneberg on Friday she hopes to do more. How we
are going to get it here remains to be seen. The other big problem
is fuel. We are continually reminded that there will be no coal this
winter and that we should lay in a store of wood in good time. Do
tell me, dear children, how and where W. and I can fell a tree?
Perhaps in the middle of the night we could murder one of the
beautiful old trees here in the Andreasstrasse, we two shrivelled-up
ancient little people? We are told that there will be warm communal meeting places in Hamburg for the freezing population, and
I can see myself crouching with a saucepan on my knees in one of
those stuffy places. I must confess I am scared stiff of the cold.

Sadly Jacoba and Fritz have postponed their visit till September.
I waited for them every minute last week. I get up at 6 o'clock
every morning. W. has to have his breakfast punctually at 7.30 and
during Maria's absence I had to see to everything. Now it has
become a habit. We have booked ourselves into the Parkhaus for
three weeks and will be there with Professor Hecke and wife. I
shall try to rest as much as I can. Hecke was very ill and had a
complicated operation, a successful one, thank goodness, and not
as serious as the doctors feared. Irmgard Lieven, who left us on
1 August, has not yet found accommodation. The billeting officer
came to see us, but thought Mimi's tiny room was not really suit-
able for letting. There are still so many homeless in desperate need
of somewhere to live, and I feel terribly guilty that we still have so
much room and comfort, when masses of others face misery. We

are never grateful enough, but believe me, we do count our blessings. It's just that we are tired and used up, we can hardly work ourselves up to any strong emotion, after all those years of tension and exhaustion, of fear and nearness of death, of eternal unrest.

I am sure it is this very feeling of being drained which makes it impossible for the German nation to rebel against their new hardships. They are totally passive, yes almost accepting, an attitude which strikes the British as most peculiar, annoys them and they think ludicrous. 'Where are all those Nazis?' they keep on asking. 'How is it that we do not encounter antagonism and difficulties? They almost welcome us with open arms!' It is not simply a complete lack of character and stamina, but a general lassitude of such dimensions that it is easier to accept and obey orders. How often in life, after a serious conflict, one gives in through sheer exhaustion, shrugs one's shoulders in an attitude of 'laisser aller'. I myself am capable of neither happiness nor sadness at the moment, I cannot get excited, I do not even hope very much. 'What the next years will bring us, I do not know, but I am afraid we shall not have much peace,' Goethe said to Eckermann. Perhaps there will be a really happy *big* surprise bringing an upsurge, a strong release of new life. To go on exercising patience, to go on feeling homesick for all of you, to go on consoling myself with nothing, my soul just refuses to accept, it is becoming dented and blunt.

Evening is descending, and in the rain-heavy grey sky there is a tiny pattern of light on the horizon, like a small rent in the gloom, promising brightness behind. Through this narrow gap one can sense a wider splendour of brilliance, not this dull, oppressive murkiness, and I wish I could pierce through it.

If Japan surrenders, will there be peace all over the world? *Peace.* I would like to write this little word over and over again, a whole page full of nothing else until I myself were filled to overflowing with peace. But this frightful atom bomb could destroy the entire world, and all that is now would be the past. There – a big flame has been lit in the sky, two more splits have torn the greyness asunder. 'To draw the curtain', to penetrate to what is truly essential, how difficult that is; one is stuck so pathetically to trivialities. Goodbye my four loved ones, and good night! The town is overrun with Tommies and ill-assorted mixed couples.

15 August, 1945.

Now there is peace throughout the whole world. I heard this morning on the radio that Japan has surrendered unconditionally. Prime Minister Attlee was making a speech, and so was President Truman. In England and the United States there are two public holidays, and in both countries boundless jubilation. For the first time ever the Japanese Emperor has addressed his country over the radio, informing the population of the surrender. The Japanese people are said to be abysmally shocked, one could hear them sobbing. They stood with bowed heads and murmured, 'Forgive us, oh Emperor, that we failed you.' I was quite beside myself listening, but what and who is a stupid little person like me compared to such an event in history? Thousands will have joined me in shedding tears of emotional relief.

The Ministry of Labour has given orders that lectures for students should start at once, and several professors have announced their programmes. Professors Lauen and Genzmar, and W. too, are going to give courses for the matriculated students. W. already gives twice-weekly lecture courses, alongside all the other work he has to do, and performs with great animation. We celebrated today's peace treaty with a dish of our last little beans and four fresh bread rolls, sitting on the balcony. My heart has hardly taken it in.

23 August, 1945.

We are at the Parkhaus again. After a dreadful day we arrived here on Monday, not until 8 o'clock in the evening, dead beat, worn out, irritable and cross. Hot and dishevelled as we were, there was a formal reception and introduction in the dining-room; 'His Magnificence, the Rector of the University of Hamburg, Professor Wolff and his lady.' Carelessly nodding to right and left, we collapsed onto our chairs and devoured the gorgeous egg-custard. We are in the same comfortable room as before with an adjoining bathroom – no hot water – and feel quite at home here. Unfortunately W. has to travel into town every morning and afternoon for his administrative duties and lectures, a constant rush which makes him look haggard. But it cannot be helped and at least he can enjoy the fresh air here and the good food, which is, however, not as plentiful as last year. Our butter ration, especially, is minute,

one can hardly see it. But W. has an extra allocation, $\frac{1}{8}$ lb. per
week, and with that and with the bread and jam which I brought,
we can have a little something in between meals. Last night at
dinner, small scallop shells of marinaded fish mixture were offered,
and when W. took one, the waitress pointed out reproachfully that
he was not entitled to a whole one! He was quite taken aback and
returned it to the dish. I am ashamed that we are so greedy. I
could eat all day long, whereas in the old days I used to propagate
the idea of taking one pill per day, containing sufficient calories
to keep one going.

There is quite a large circle of people here, all in need of
recuperation, all so-called upper-class society. Our old friend
Hecke has the corner table. He looks very poorly, quite decimated
after his serious operation, forty pounds lighter than before and
without his beloved *embonpoint*. Next to him are his wife and her
friend, an elderly spinster, who calls Hecke 'our little Professor',
and with Frau Hecke fusses over him non-stop with cushions and
rugs, encouraging remarks and small titbits. It makes W. squirm,
but Hecke seems to like it. In the opposite corner sits Frau
Schlinck, looking delicate, pale and sad, and her companion
Fräulein Siebel. They have been here for months, ever since her
husband died, and the British have commandeered her entire
house. We are particularly fond of her. In solitary splendour Herr
Leiser lords it over his table, full of ruddy health and joviality. He
has a kind word for everybody and regales us with anecdotes from
his successful business life. He does not think the meals are quite
what they should be, but he knows of many secret channels through
which a variety of little extras are available. The other day, in
exchange for a camera, he obtained I do not know how much
butter, sugar and flour. In the centre of the dining-room, at a
much larger table, we have the regal proprietress Frau Selig with
her sister and daughter. From this vantage point she can control
our behaviour and supervise what in her view constitutes a most
advantageous way of getting better, of regaining our health. She
patted W.'s emaciated cheek and he shrank away from her pitying
touch. But he controlled himself, and even managed a smile in
response to her patronizing glance. Her sister, a former teacher, is
a gentle, kindly, elderly spinster, somewhat overshadowed by Frau
Selig. But the daughter, Fräulein Leni, is *'une beauté du diable'*,
night-dark raven locks, fiery eyes, ostentatious make-up, strong

perfume and slightly provocative behaviour. I am fond of her and
she likes me, admires W. and goes into raptures about our 'charming' flat. I don't know why, except that we are perhaps less
conventional than the other people here. I am alone a good deal,
because W. has to be out so often. I do not mind, I read, write and
sew, and also prepare my lessons.

My two pupils came yesterday, soaked by the rain and indeed
barefoot, since they have only one pair of shoes each. We worked
hard and I steered them through the thirteenth century right up to
Chaucer. We talked mainly about Langland, Gower and Wycliffe.
I suppose I can assume that you know who they are? I have only
just made their acquaintance! And the world? The weather continues to be grey, damp, drizzly and autumnal. Hamburg is without
vegetables and fruit, rations are minimal, partly cut again, and
there is hardly any sugar or cereals. Maria goes on preserving
what she can get at her sister's in Etz, and I sacrificed my lovely
heavy walking-boots in this good cause. If you want to get anything
laundered these days, you have to contribute briquettes, the same
at the hairdresser's, and we haven't got any. Through a kind
recommendation from Professor Kroetz we had two cwt. of coal
delivered. A man came at dusk. If questions were asked we were
to say the coal was a gift from a bombed-out cellar. Secretly
and in silence I had to press a considerable tip into his black
hand. At least we have got this small store now and, judging
from the amount of money I paid by way of a tip, I dare
to hope that some more will come in due course. If we do
not die of cold this winter, we shall have bridged a considerable
chasm.

Your cousin Wilhelm Sieveking has been appointed headmaster
of the big grammar school for boys, the Johanneum. Schlensog is
headmaster of the primary school in Nienstädten. It is said that
there are still many Nazis in hiding, leading a gluttonous existence
in secret, probably the very people who ostentatiously denounced
their neighbours and then themselves carried on cheating, defraud-
ing and illegally hoarding. And yet masses of questionnaires are
being issued, which have to be filled in. People are put into cate-
gories, are examined and dismissed. W. is beginning to know a
number of English people and enjoys some of his new acquaintances. He has been invited to go to England; someone drew his
portrait; somebody else is going to get him a subscription to *The*

Times, and yet another has taken a letter for you, Ruth. They have arranged for a stenographer to sit in on his lectures and translate them because they are interested in what he has to say.

16 September, 1945.

We have been back in Hamburg for a week. I feel really rested and well fed, but W. is neither, alas. There was far too much rushing about for him, and the reproachful glances from her ladyship, Frau Selig, when he was late for practically every meal, reduced his enjoyment of the plentiful and tasty food. Your poor stepfather's life is very bothersome. Everyone seeks him out, wants his advice or opinion, and yet there are always difficulties and intrigues being spun, especially by the medical professorial staff at the Eppendorf Hospital. I often feel so desperately sorry for him when he returns home, exhausted and disheartened, looking so grey and old. There are quite a few Englishmen who are sympathetic and interested, but they do not understand his situation, nor the general sorry plight. We are, after all, the vanquished foe, despised culprits who can be ordered about to their hearts' content. Often this is almost impossible to bear, and perhaps we should be allowed a little more freedom and self-determination, otherwise, beneath the surface of obedience, there might be a new growth of hatred and resentment, jeopardizing the desired co-existence. Decisions about dismissals are constantly vetoed. No sooner has a complicated case been sorted out than those in power reject the resolution and work has to start again, right from the beginning, torture for the person concerned and also for the Rector.

On the whole we had three good weeks in Hochkamp. I had a lot of visitors in the afternoons, when punctually at 4 o'clock coffee was served in our room, generally quite decent cake as well. We succumbed to the temptation and bought a pound of butter for 200 marks from Ruth's former friend, Frau Schlinck's son. Other people bought two or three pounds. How quickly one loses the habit of scraping butter. I must confess that occasionally we even put butter on our cake. One can hardly control this unnatural greed for fat and sugar. But this select circle at the Parkhaus did not really suit the present time. In a way it was quite good to go back to old customs, to remind oneself how things had been in the past. But that past is such a very long time ago, and we shabby, hungry people no longer fit into it. The general tone of conversation, the arrogant, snobbish and rather empty level of talk, was irritating. In this the Heckes completely agreed with us.

Frau Schlensog's daily visits were delightful. She cycled over, bare-legged, her white hair streaming behind her, and looked lovely. In spite of everything, both she and her husband manage to rise above all the misery. They make music together and live on an elevated *niveau,* created by themselves and out of reach for most. We went to their house with the Heckes on our last evening, and they performed his most recent composition, a quartet for two violins, a recorder and piano. The recorder soared above the other instruments, and Frau Schlensog looked like an ageless Pan, a slender figure clad in black silk with a delicate white head. Hecke did his best to regain his erstwhile corpulent figure. He appeared at every meal with a small basket over his arm, containing extra titbits, which annoyed Frau Selig quite uncommonly. Professors are a strange breed!

Thinking of all the awful things which go on outside, one cannot tolerate an existence like the Parkhaus one for more than three weeks. Many families are homeless and without the most essential prerequisites for basic living. A professorial colleague of W.'s who has lost everything in Berlin cannot find anywhere to live with his wife, quite apart from getting himself a decent suit to wear at an interview for a job. He has become an undertaker and writes cynically that, when he has finished making coffins for his wife and himself, they will end it all. In the small town in the Lausitz, where Marlene and Karin went to school, 110 people have committed suicide; old women and young girls, regardless of age, were raped by the Russians, heaven knows how often. At the Parkhaus we were introduced to Traudi Gravenhorst, the writer. She told us of unbelievable bestialities perpetrated by the Russians and her escape was a saga of horror. She is middle-aged, far from beautiful, and ill, but nonetheless was in constant danger of sexual assault. In the village where she was hiding, she could hear the screams of desperate women night after night. Not even a little six-year-old girl was spared this atrocity.

To raise a smile from you, I will tell you the following anecdote: You will remember Dr Schütt, W.'s female co-professor; she is also somewhat reduced in size and white-haired. When she went for a walk along the Elbe, she was accosted by a young British officer who suggested a little canoodle in the bushes, and she retorted in great indignation, 'Young man, I could be your granny!'

Never has the black market blossomed more profusely than now, even more so since it has been officially forbidden. Bartering is permitted and shop windows display items for exchange, while the population flatten their noses against the glass. My lovely walking-boots have gone in exchange for fuel that Maria's sister needed to do our preserves; Gustav Heinrich's army boots have been exchanged for an electric stove. My beloved little cot is going to my hairdresser Frau Rädecke to harbour her fat little Heinz, but only temporarily, because I am still hoping to see one of my own grand-children in it. She has promised me flour and cereals in return.

How different the world looked at this time last year. Gone is that overpowering and nerve-destroying unrest, the tension, the immediate proximity of death, the coming to terms with ultimate annihilation outside and inside. Instead we have this all-pervading tiredness, a passive lassitude, no redeeming feeling of freedom, no life-giving happiness. There is too much dire need, too much suffering and destruction, a perpetual cruel reminder of what we went through. Only when I am entirely by myself and listening to Beethoven, can I fall on my knees and thank God from the bottom of my heart for our deliverance.

Whenever there are letters from you, I almost choke with gladness. My frightening anxiety about you, my intolerable impatience to see you have now turned into humble gratitude and surprise that I am so truly blessed. I sometimes think that even seeing you and holding you again can hardly be of deeper beauty than my inner knowledge of you. Thank you a million times for your love and faith.

2 October, 1945.

It is a long time since I came to you, my darling children, but you are not quite so distant as you used to be, since I can correspond with Ruth and also send occasional letters to Jella in Copenhagen. Should I stop writing these diary-letters? Or shall I carry on till we meet again? I need not keep anything back from you now. My letters are carried by friendly, reliable messengers, and I am free to tell you everything that happened during those six long and hard years of war, when we waited for the end of all the horrors and hoped against hope, when we were hungry and cold, had every last bit of personal freedom snatched from us, were made into slaves, slaves of uneducated, foul-mouthed, benighted and megalo-maniac scoundrels. But perhaps future generations will be interested to know how our Military Government came into being and developed, and how slowly, very slowly, tiny, hardly visible, new seeds of hope appear in our poor, destroyed Germany, how from the barren ruins signs of an indomitable fresh life are peeping through. Hamburg is generally regarded as an oasis compared with other cities and we realize more and more how fortunate we are to live in the British zone. Many charming Englishmen visit us, every one of them prepared to carry letters. One even brought a marvellous parcel from you, Ruth dear. His name was Evans too.

25 October, 1945.

Strangely enough I am still drawn to this manuscript, although I can write and tell you everything and we are no longer hamstrung by the censor. Letters from Jella and Ruth are my greatest blessing, but I am still longing vainly for a word from Thys. You have all come so much nearer again, yet when I stretch out my arms there is still only emptiness.

Last year we thought we had reached the climax of privation, but now it looks as if we have to anticipate an even worse winter this year. We have *no coal at all* now and unless we get a small iron stove, promised by one of Jacoba's co-patients, we will have to freeze. It is called a 'witch-furnace', stands on four small legs, and would have to be installed in the library with the pipe going out through the window, not exactly a thing of beauty. The prospect of cold, hunger and dirt – no soap or hot water – is not pleasant. The electricity ration, 2.7 kilowatts per day, is so meagre that one can neither iron nor cook. W., when he is at home, climbs onto a chair every five minutes to read the meter. At 10 o'clock it is 'lights out and bed!' Homely comfort is a thing of the past. We sit in overcoats with blankets round our legs, and up till now it has been bearable because we have not had any frost as yet, in fact the weather this autumn has been rather mild. Thank goodness we have got some wood. Our friends the von Gosslers have given us a big beech tree, and a fortnight ago a lorry arrived and decanted the enormous logs onto the pavement outside our house. Maria and

I had to shift the big pile into the cellar, which took us four hours, causing sore hands and tired backs. Fritz kept guard, so that nothing would be stolen while we carted and tidied the wood in the cellar, and several little street urchins helped, earning an apple and one mark. When the logs crackle and spit in the kitchen range they make a lovely comforting sound and we all congregate in the kitchen. One did not know how fortunate one was in the old days.

I mentioned a co-patient of Jacoba's! Yes, your poor sister arrived three weeks ago with a high temperature and was admitted to Professor Kroetz's hospital in Altona the following day. To begin with we thought it was an attack of typhoid fever, but it was hepatitis, which is slowly getting better. She is terribly run down, has lost twelve pounds in weight and was very poorly. She is improving bit by bit, but has been advised to take at least another month off work. She will probably come to us on Monday to recuperate and be nursed by me. Her stay in hospital has become very unpleasant since our friend Professor Kroetz was dismissed from his position at a moment's notice. She shares a ward with two ladies, both seriously ill with heart disease. Fritz and I cannot visit her every day, because of the immense transport difficulties. Every time we have to battle furiously to get onto a tram, shoving, squeezing, pushing and squashing, and the other day we walked all the way back from Altona in pouring rain.

16 November, 1945.
Jacoba has been with us for two and a half weeks already and is slowly recovering. We have a strange and in many respects completely different sort of time behind us, are always glad to be together from morn till night, and are once again sharing a lot of sadness and happiness. The sadness is due to discomfort. It is icy cold throughout the flat except for the kitchen, where in the reduced range the von Gossler logs are crackling and popping, thawing out our swollen fingers and frozen noses. Whenever anyone opens the door, icy draughts creep in, and we prefer the pong of six cooped-up people to any kind of fresh air. My W. sits at the head of the kitchen table, his pipe steaming away; Fritzchen plays a word game and makes funny faces, not allowed to talk and hating the silence; Maria is darning her pyjamas, cursing her fate; Jacoba and I write letters in very close proximity. And then dear Tante Lulu

pops her head in and looks like a frightened little chicken. Somebody has wantonly taken far too many coupons from her ration book and she is beside herself with worry. She has become much more feeble in body and soul latterly and is now a truly old woman. So it is primarily the cold which makes our day-to-day existence such a sad state of affairs, especially early in the morning and late at night. It is barely dawn when I have to creep out of my cocoon on the chaise-longue where I try to keep warm while Jacoba has my bed. It is quite an art to get into it. I wrap myself up and tuck myself in, and yet, if a blanket slides off, the cold insinuates itself up my body, despite the fact that I wear a dressing-gown, woolly pants, two pairs of stockings and a head-scarf, and my nose has to be under the covers. But I like waking up, knowing that Jacoba is so near to me, and soon Fritzchen's bright voice shouts '*Mutt*', his footsteps grope towards her bed and he crawls in on the warm side of his mother. The bathroom is just as cold, and personal hygiene somewhat problematic without a drop of hot water. It is strange for me to surrender my personal vanity, to give up painstaking cleanliness, but why not? We wear only our oldest clothes all day long, coats on top, and nobody cares what one looks like. The only things which everyone gets worked up about are the topical questions, 'Have you any coal? Have you any potatoes? Can you manage on the bread ration? Do you know where to get extra butter?' The black market is the focal point of fascination for all. We have already spent about 1,000 marks on 2 lbs. of dripping at 130 marks per pound; 2 lbs. of butter at 250 marks per pound; 4 lbs. of sugar at 40-50 marks per pound; and today Jacoba has ordered 10 lbs. of flour at 25 marks per pound and 2 more pounds of fat at 175 marks per pound. Money is of no consequence whatsoever, all that matters is nourishment and survival through the impending winter months of cold, famine and the risk of serious epidemics. If we survive this winter we can bless our lucky stars. In his capacity as Rector, W. has made an official request to the Senate for a stove plus five metres of pipe and three knee-hinges. This stove is to adorn our library, the exhaust fumes being directed through a hole in the window.

It is a pity that you cannot have a peep at our odd communal life in the narrow kitchen. You would have to guess at the identities of the bent heads, one bald, two grey, two fair and one tinged with white. Jacoba and I have to laugh sometimes when we imagine

your astonished and incredulous eyes. 'You look like an old
Bedouin woman,' Jacoba says to me when I get into bed. But my
bare neck and arms are more like a concentration camp victim's.
Not exactly a pretty sight. Nor is your sister restored in herself in
any sense, yet she is always full of sympathetic kindness, willing to
help, and in my opinion already much too eager to do things. I
fetched her in a horse-drawn carter's wagon, a clattering vehicle in
which Fritz and I sat swaying precariously with the driver, she on
a box in the back, pulled by a pathetically lean little nag. She was
on her back in bed for a fortnight, and I sat with her practically
all the time, either reading aloud, talking or darning, swathed in
blankets. Now she is up again, revelling in the kitchen warmth
with us all. She walks over to Lanka in the mornings to have a
new coat made. Lanka, my blind friend Frau Schneider's daughter,
has reopened her dressmaking business in the Binderstrasse atelier
under new management. They work only four hours each day, for
after that their fingers get too cold and stiff. Jacoba has also been
to see the Medical Association, has visited old patients and new
friends, and she never comes home empty-handed, they all give
her what they can spare. She is quite indefatigable, planning for
Fritz and herself, and the boy is always good-tempered and in high
spirits, and except when he has to do his lessons, attentive, happy
and exceptionally capable. Never too tired to run errands, he knows
all about public transport, carries heavy loads and returns home
with quite a variety of things, a big head of cabbage or some
bartered potatoes. We have not had potatoes for many weeks, only
fifty pounds of swedes as a substitute, and one gets used to that too.

Last year we thought we had reached the limit of our endurance
as far as the dark grimness of winter was concerned, but really it
is much much worse this year, except for the absence of air raids –
and heaven be praised for that : we are no longer in deadly peril
night and day. But the question of food has *never* been so critical
as it is now. We literally eat nothing but cabbage and swedes and,
if we are lucky, thin porridge made with skim milk. Each person
has half a litre of skim milk per week. How is one to give just that
little bit extra to a person recovering from a severe illness? We
have no eggs, no full milk, 200 grammes of butter per month and
150 grammes of meat. If so many people were not much worse off,
one would despair. Still, you learn something new every day. Your
stepfather is an example of total frugality and forbearance. How

he would have abhorred this kitchen existence in the old days, side by intimate side with grumpy Maria! But he never says a word, is invariably kind and considerate. I am not! I often find the situation quite intolerable.

The bright and joyful moments during these dark weeks were the arrival of many letters from Ruth, fewer but equally dear ones from Jella, and also parcels big and small. We break into peals of happy exclamations when the doorbell goes and another Englishman appears and climbs up the stairs. We had three in one day the other week, and every one of them brought quite miraculous things. Nearly all my desires were fulfilled, even a comb, shoe-laces, soap, matches and chocolate. Fritz hoards everything in little boxes and just looks at them lovingly about ten times a day; his grandmother cannot do that. People here are also very kind and bring apples, for instance, and we talk about tempting dishes until we nearly cry. Since it gets dark at 4 o'clock, we hardly ever go out after that, and each one seeks out his or her warm little corner. A patient of Gustav Heinrich's brought us a small sack of anthracite yesterday, which made such a beautiful bright fire that we all had hot-water bottles for our beds. Enough for today. I do not know whether I have painted a sufficiently animated picture of our November days in the year 1945 for you. I hope so. Farewell my dears.

January 1946.
My last account was in November, and now it is January and perhaps we have the worst of this cruellest of all winters behind us. Now I can write to all of you direct and without difficulties and you will know what it is like here. Perhaps now I shall put a final full-stop to these letters, since they no longer serve a purpose. I have reiterated all our misery *ad nauseam* probably, have moaned too much, and you, my loved ones, have reacted with patient love and concern. Letters and parcels have come in veritable showers of merciful relief, and we are almost well off now. My store cupboard is filled with tins containing delicious things, even tea and coffee; cocoa and chocolate are no longer unobtainable rarities. But the very best is still receiving your letters. They have brought you so much nearer and have increased my longing to see you.

We are still short of fuel and often very cold, but we are able to gather around a small stove in the library in the evenings. We all suffer from chilblains, but so does everybody else. I sleep in W.'s den, my own room is like an ice-rink with mildew on the walls. Many kind Britishers come to see us, always with some friendly gift, and we are particularly fond of Mr Price, Major Kelly, Captain Evans and Mr Poston, and there are many more. Communications between Aberystwyth and Hamburg fly backwards and forwards. Jacoba is still in Neustadt, a caring and faithful executant of a difficult job. She looks after us with unending love. W. had a bad hunger oedema, but he is better now and eats with colossal appetite as many meals as I can give him. I am still the same impatient and not always very lovable creature, hate the cold of the early morning, waste much of the day pottering around, and only become an acceptable human being with slightly more profound interests after tea. 'I do not know why I am not a bit nicer!'

God bless you all. Farewell.

Mother.

Epilogue by Ruth Evans

'You will have to come and see for yourself,' Tilli Wolff-Möncke-berg wrote on 18 July, 1945, and I did go to see for myself not so very long after her last entry in January 1946.

Fortunately we, 'the far-away children', apart from our brother Jan, were all alive and well, were able to bring back into her life the happiness and renewed hope she had longed for so passionately and patiently. It is important to remember that during the year 1946 we were still not permitted to conduct an ordinary postal correspondence, that written contact between Great Britain and Germany was possible only through the kind conveyance of letters by hand through friends in Control Commission and the Armed Forces. My brother Thys, living in the United States, did not have this advantage, and the initial messages from him and his wife had to pass through my hands before they reached Tilli and Emil Wolff.

At the end of October 1946 I was able to travel to Hamburg, a journey I shall not easily forget. Since ordinary travel facilities did not then exist I managed, not without difficulties, to enter occupied Western Germany as a war correspondent and reported my observations and experiences to various newspapers in Great Britain. After an absence of eight years the impact of what I saw was traumatic. I flew out from a military airport in Hampshire to Bückeberg in Westphalia in a converted Dakota hospital-plane with bucket-seats and camouflaged portholes. Never having flown before, I was very nervous and my state of intense agitation was increased by the unaccustomed khaki uniform I was wearing and the company of several fairly high-ranking British officers who shared this long and bumpy flight. It was very cold and the first night in a Nissen hut on a snow-covered field only increased my discomfort and apprehension. The following day I travelled to Hamburg in a battered, unheated Volkswagen, driven by a very young German prisoner of war, who was on parole for these services. He disappeared as soon as he had delivered me at the Correspondents' Mess where I was to stay, and I never saw him again. Our entry into the city of Hamburg took my breath away. Nearly all the familiar landmarks from the past had gone, and had it not been for the two rivers, the Elbe and the Alster, I would not have known where I was. Typical Hamburg autumn weather, a

murky grey fog and drizzling rain, did not help. We drove up
the Mönckebergstrasse, the broad shopping street named after my
grandfather, past strange, unrecognizable heaps of rubble and
people who were walking like grey shadows over a vast cemetery.
The glass dome on the big main station was just a skeleton of steel
girders, twisted and shapeless.

That same afternoon I made my way on foot to the Andreasstrasse. It had not been possible to inform my family of the exact
date and time of my arrival. I knew of course that their house had
escaped destruction, but the full realization of the chaos all around
them was a terrible shock. My knees were shaking, my khaki beret
seemed to be sticking to my forehead as I climbed up the stairs to
the third storey of that tall block of flats, skirting sandbags and heaps
of fallen plaster. As children and long afterwards we had used a
phrase of music from Brahms' first symphony as our family whistle.
I stood outside the front door of the flat and composed myself
sufficiently to force my lips around the little snatch of tune. I
heard a gasp and a clatter. My mother, who was entertaining two
old school-friends for tea, had dropped the plate she was carrying.
The door flew open and we were in each other's arms after seven
and a half long years.

My first thought was how small and thin she had become. We
had always been the same size, but now I towered above her and
her body seemed very frail. Her two friends, one of them the Frau
von Gossler mentioned in her letters, left tactfully. Next it was my
stepfather, my sister Jacoba and the quite incredibly altered, big
boy Fritz whose hands and faces I was touching, speech so far
being hardly possible. Their incredulous laughter at my British
uniform helped to restore some kind of balance, and soon there was
a fresh pot of tea and biscuits from an American CARE parcel.
Pappi Wolff, as I had always called him, sat, as of old, in his
big armchair in the library, smiling blissfully behind a cloud of
smoke from his pipe filled with English tobacco, and Fritzchen
stuffed his mouth with NAAFI chewing-gum. In those early
moments of reunion it was as if I had never been 'on the other
side'.

How they survived I need not report. Apart from the inevitable
and tragic losses the family had sustained, like innumerable other
families throughout Europe and overseas, we had been unbelievably
lucky. Only slowly did the significance of the lack of communication during the war years catch up with us, and certain gaps in our
knowledge of each other were never quite filled. One had to start
afresh, to try to understand the consequences of individual suffer-

ing. It was necessary to bridge the gulf of surmise, prejudice and half-knowledge about the origins and unavoidable outcome of this world disaster.

As I wandered through the streets of Hamburg during the three weeks of my stay, I was continually at a loss how to envisage the future. I had grave doubts about whether the German members of my family would ever be robust and healthy again. And Hamburg, would this old city ever recover her tough and independent spirit, would this ruined town ever be rebuilt? I doubted that too. Destruction on the scale exhibited there has literally to be seen to be believed. It cannot be conceived by the ordinary imagination. An area the size of Birmingham had been razed to the ground, suburb after suburb had been wiped out. Miraculously the centre of Hamburg was relatively unscathed and I even found parts that on the surface looked much the same as when I had last seen them. But while they had been clean and tidy then, now they had degenerated into evil-smelling slums, incredibly overcrowded. Generally, however, Hamburg was unrecognizable; street after street of burnt-out houses, rubble, twisted girders, with only a small pathway in the middle of an erstwhile thoroughfare to let the vehicles through. Most of the familiar landmarks had vanished : factories, houses, churches, schools, hospitals – which ghastly ruin belonged to which? Not a living soul in the streets, no trees, no birds, not even a stray dog or cat. Nothing.

It was a city of the dead. During the heavy raids of 1943, which all took place between the Sunday and Thursday of one week – a period generally known as 'The Catastrophe' – more than 30,000 people were killed in Hamburg. The figure is an approximation, because counting was almost impossible during this period of complete chaos. Some accounts put it at nearer 50,000. Thousands fled and never returned; many were killed on the roads as they tried to escape. Vast areas were sealed off immediately after the raids and under the collapsed buildings lay thousands of corpses, the authorities not daring to reopen these natural graves.

Several times I paused and just stood. The air was quiet, yet one imagined shrill cries vibrating through the stillness. High up on a pile of rubble was a clothes-line, a few bits of washing flapping in the wind. A sign of life! Avidly my eyes searched for others. Yes, over there, a thin trail of smoke, and down there, in the cellar of a burnt-out ruin, a flowerpot in a tiny window. Was it possible that people still lived there? An old man picked his way slowly over a pile of bricks, occasionally stooping to pick up small pieces of wood. Was this really Mittelstrasse, where not so long ago crowds had thronged the pavements and filled the shops? Yes, it was, for there was the street name hanging crookedly from a tumbled down wall. When I looked up the old man had vanished into a hole in the ground.

What did they feel, these ghosts who roamed the former streets of the city? I tried to talk to former friends and acquaintances, but each time I came up against a barrier, not of language, that was no problem, rather something deeper and more fundamental. I was one of the victors, and of course I was wearing their uniform. No one wanted to talk except to repeat the story of their own suffering, and what I wished to find out had to be extracted more by innuendo than by direct conversation. I tried to explain that we in Britain had known disillusionment, weariness and exhaustion, too. But not one of the people I talked to in Hamburg was aware or even wanted to be aware of the heavy price we had paid, the privations we had suffered, the losses we had sustained. Perhaps this was not surprising; there were not many at home in Great Britain who fully comprehended that, apart from the obvious calamity of total war and the hardships caused by eventual defeat, a number of Germans had also had to face the dilemma of an almost schizophrenic split between love for their homeland and disgust with its rulers, whom they had tolerated, even condoned, at best on the grounds of patriotism.

Prejudices and antagonism were rife, my motives for coming misunderstood, and the blame for the outcome of the war was shifted from shoulder to shoulder. Nor did the regulations concerning non-fraternization help. My fellow war correspondents considered me naïvely officious. My family wanted me to be with them, afraid that I would be unduly distressed and fatigued. In the end I turned, inevitably, to my stepfather, who never recoiled from answering my questions, even though at times they must have been very painful for him.

Emil Wolff was far from well. As Rector – Vice-Chancellor – of the University of Hamburg, he had the almost impossible task of combining tricky and virtually insoluble problems of administration with the running of his own department, which, for lack of staff, needed him to give lectures and seminars, to set and mark examinations. Compared with Great Britain, food supplies were of a lesser and lower standard. I must freely admit that I found the meals in the Andreasstrasse very unpalatable, their mainstay of cereal – coarse-ground or bruised corn-cuttings, which were made into dumplings or a kind of porridge – almost inedible, despite grumpy Maria's strenuous efforts to disguise the coarseness. She really did her best to prepare appetizing dishes, loved to be praised, but only the contents of parcels from overseas added a little delicacy. No wonder Tilli, who before the war had never given food more than a passing thought, was so preoccupied with nourishment. Emil Wolff had suffered from hunger oedema, his legs, feet and hands were still swollen, and an additional irritation was eczema on his head, caused by lack of vitamins. Despite these unpleasant handicaps, he prepared, while I was there, two formal orations to be presented at the official inauguration of the new academic year. He sat till late at night in his cold den, hands in mittens, a scarf wound round his neck, his feet on a hot-water bottle, surrounded by files, books and papers, and was hardly aware of his unfavourable surroundings. I went to the ceremony and well remember my discomfiture as, in my uniform, I followed the retinue of the head of Control Commission into the hall. When we entered the entire audience rose in respect, my parents amongst them.

During that time Emil Wolff was sometimes offered bribes, which offended rather than tempted him, for he thought they undermined his integrity. His administrative duties included the fraught and complex business of de-Nazification. People, anxious to retain their positions or wanting to establish themselves in new employment, were not beyond offering recompense in kind for favouritism or preferential treatment. Tilli was sorely tried when, for instance, a fat goose was brought to the flat under cover of night by the father of a student who wanted to matriculate, and this offering was rejected with disdain. She worried about my step-father's health, about my sister's frailty and Fritz's need for extra nourishment. Despite the fact that she herself weighed barely eighty pounds, she seemed better able to cope with the near starvation diet once her desperate hunger for us children had been somewhat stilled. When freedom of speech and action had been restored to the Professor, he regained much of his former enterprise and stamina in the academic and intellectual sense, while Tilli's inherent and lovable vanity revived remarkably once she knew she was going to meet outsiders again. She often speaks in her letters of the many and consistent power cuts and they were still in force when I came. During that very chilly autumn of 1946 she regularly got up before 6 o'clock in the morning, dressed, did her hair and made up while there was still electric light (it was switched off an hour later), and not once did I see her slovenly or ill-kempt. She set an example to the others, who, under the circumstances, might easily have let themselves go. The spirit of the 'Hamburg State

Princess' was still very much alive in her. Although all her clothes were seven or more years old, had been altered, darned and repaired, stored away, covered with ashes, water and sand, she still managed to look regal, which was more than one could say of many a human shadow one encountered in the streets. Both Emil and Tilli were nearing their seventieth year. Their spirit was exceptional, they not only faced, but measured up to the difficulties they encountered and, by that time, had gone a long way towards making the best of them.

In May 1946 Emil Wolff had been asked by the European Service of the BBC to take part in a series of lectures on 'The European Tradition'. He was pleased and flattered to be in the company of T. S. Eliot and Karl Barth, the former speaking before him, the latter after him. He sent me a draft of this lecture at the same time. In it he writes : 'War with weapons has ended, war which led to unconditional victory by those who fought for freedom and tradition and were united in their aim. But the fight for the continuity and fruitful extension of our European heritage has only just begun. All will now depend on the outcome of this endeavour, whether we can expect a true renaissance of a new and productive life in Europe, or whether we will have to accept a final degeneration, a descent into nonentity, pushed into subservience by those mighty powers who rule the other continents, a state experienced by the Greeks under the imperialism of Rome. The struggle to maintain European traditions and European thought processes, conceived originally by the Greeks, is shared by everybody who is still able to understand their meaning and is convinced of their life-giving significance. It makes no difference who bears the torch or whence it will be carried. It remains our duty to prevent the flickering light from being extinguished during the present darkness and storm, to shelter it gently and to rekindle its brightness. And this duty falls equally heavily on the German nation and on the sons of our European sister-nations. Indeed we have to recapture our rich and noble tradition. It is wrong to postulate that our dire necessity to procure the basic tenets of existence must needs take all our strength and all our resources. One can counter the old saying "Living precedes Philosophizing" by affirming that the rebuilding of our outward circumstances can only be achieved when our inner life has been rebalanced; the one depends on the other.

'A new, meaningful form of German democracy cannot be achieved merely by the introduction of a reorganized constitution and the creation of an economic and social order based on external justice. Both these premises can gain strength and life only if they take root in well-founded motivation towards the re-establishment of a common will to succeed. In remembering what conditioned the historical development of German ideology, it will become apparent that, despite its very individual stamp, it is nonetheless part of the European heritage, indivisible from the universal concatenation of ideas, intricately intertwined with all European nations, dependent on giving and receiving spiritual stimulation and guidance and part of the growth process of the unique European tradition.

'A warning that a reawakening of the universal European spirit is essential must go to all members of the European community, but first and foremost to Germany. It is a challenge to the intrinsic nature of Germany to return to its true self. By surrendering herself to an all-embracing ideology, Germany is given the opportunity to find her way back from her most gruesome isolation and self-estrangement into the realm of thought which constituted her true origin.'

In 1946 this was a courageous, prophetic and yet almost completely lost cry from the wilderness. Then, as in pre-war days, Emil Wolff's lectures were packed to capacity, almost to bursting point, with students eager to imbibe his quietly spoken words; but also with people who were simply looking for a place of warmth and rest and a snooze. Everyone was tired and confused, and very few had his intellectual stamina. That winter Hamburg University admitted 3,400 students out of a total of approximately 7,000 applicants. Seventy per cent were men, most of them ex-servicemen. Selection was difficult here too, the process of de-Nazification meant much concentrated work for those who had to consider each individual case. Staff and students alike were working against heavy odds. Most Hamburg professors had lost all their books and equipment during the heavy raids of 1943. Many had retired or had died during the war, and successors had not yet been appointed. The main University buildings were badly damaged in 1945 and could not be used. Problems of accommodation were increased by the incorporation of the University of the Baltic provinces. Apart from these external causes of confusion, each reinstated member of staff had to face and overcome not only his own weariness and exhaustion, but also the untrained, disordered minds of the young students and the strains of readjustment in the older ones. The teaching of the rudiments of self-expression, unhampered by fear and suspicion, was complicated by the fact that hardly anyone had learned as yet to rid himself of the formless entanglements of Nazi ideology. Older people in Great Britain and

Germany alike held the view that the subtle poison of indoctrination and lies, which still snared the minds of German post-war students, could not be eradicated until contact with the outside world was re-established on a large scale. As long as people were forced to remain in isolation, with no chance of seeing beyond the frontiers of their own personal struggles, re-education was virtually impossible. The door to freedom of speech and freedom of action had to be reopened. But only those like Emil Wolff who positively and not nostalgically cherished the memory of past experiences, could look through that door with hope and expectation. Most others would hesitate on the threshold and shrink from precipitating themselves into a new void of unknown quality. They felt the instinctive need of a guiding hand to lead them through, but dared not display their ignorance by asking for they knew not what, nor their prejudices well fostered by the Hitler régime.

One cold November day I had lunch with some students in the 'Mensa', the University refectory. There was no heating and everyone in this cheerless icy room with boarded-up windows sat wrapped up in threadbare coats, mufflers and blankets. Silently they spooned up their equally threadbare stew, while their breath trailed through the room like thin smoke. My thoughts went to the College in Wales I had recently left, to the noisy gathering of relatively healthy and certainly vigorous ex-service students at their midday meal. The contrast was striking. Here as there the percentage of ex-servicemen was high. Many British ex-servicemen looked tired and strained, but there was not the grim hopelessness which seemed to be carved into the features of this hungry, silent and conspicuously maimed group of Germans, who, one supposed, were once young. It is no exaggeration to say that only one student in a hundred had a room to himself to sleep and work in, and even if he had, there was no fuel to make it comfortable. Most of them had to work at the same time as pursuing their academic studies. From overcrowded billets, provided for some of the refugees and homeless by student-relief organizations, they had to do what jobs they could find to earn a meagre subsistence allowance. Night-watching in partly destroyed business premises was at a premium; cutting wood and carting coal; demolition work; running errands – not for money, but for the odd sandwich. The struggle to survive was often far too strenuous for them to contemplate even a minimum of academic studies to pass examinations. And yet the incentive of guaranteed employment for a number of years to come helped to make the standard of examination results astonishingly high, despite the harsh circumstances of daily life.

After my return home to Wales my mother wrote to me on 18 November, 1946 : 'Over and over again I have to tell you what it meant to us that you came. Somehow new courage, new hope and a new *joie de vivre* have entered into our home, and yet also the threatening thought of all the things that happened to each of us during those long and heartbreaking years of separation.'

Tilli's innate sensitivity, rooted in her love for her children, was victorious in the end. She believed and trusted and therefore she understood. If I had ever feared that 'being enemies' would separate us in any way, she dispelled all anxieties by putting round me once again the mantle of her unchanging concern and affection. In February 1947 she and my stepfather came to Great Britain. In Wales it was the coldest winter in living memory. For weeks on end a thick blanket of snow lay right to the edge of the Irish Sea and many inland roads were totally impassable. While Emil Wolff embarked on a lengthy study trip, Tilli came to Aberystwyth, eagerly expected by the grandchildren she had never seen. We were joined by my eldest sister, Jella, and her youngest son. That part of the family, after their flight to Sweden, had returned to Denmark at the end of the war. A reunion with my one surviving brother in America was yet to come. It was not an easy winter. We were short of food and fuel. But Tilli rested and recovered to a remarkable degree and enjoyed every moment of her stay. She was amazed and delighted by the unprejudiced welcome she was given by everyone she met and spoke freely about her experiences. In fact our friends came flocking with gifts and tokens of affection, and a meeting between her and a friend of ours whose son was killed in the war was very touching.

Our combined anxiety was concentrated on her husband. He eventually joined us in Wales after a strenuous tour of British universities and colleges. It was immediately obvious that he had overtaxed himself to the point of almost complete exhaustion. He had come with doubts and misgivings, yet spurred by the necessity of re-establishing contacts in the academic field and motivated by his great love for all that the Anglo-Saxon world stood for in the past. We used to tease him about his almost unqualified admiration for everything British, from Worcester sauce to Shakespeare. But this, his first visit to Great Britain after the war, was so shattering an experience that despite all our gentle persuasion and pressure he never came again. It was difficult then, no easier now, to analyse his depression. He was conscious of his ill-health, of the shabbiness of his clothes, of the compromises the Hitler régime had forced upon him, of a reluctance to reiterate confessions of faith in things which no longer seemed to exist. He was conscious of the fact that being one of the first, if not the first, German professor to visit British institutions of learning after the war, he would have to formulate his observations in a most careful manner not to be mis-understood, not to be pitied, not to be regarded as hopelessly nostalgic, out of date and out of touch, as an ancient liberal re-actionary. He nearly died of shame when a kindly lady academic offered to darn his pullover; he resented the fact that a glass of her sherry made him dizzy; that he could no longer sit up in a cold room and lead a discussion till the early hours of the morning; that speaking English was not as easy as it had been. He was tired and undernourished, lacked that amazing Jack-in-the-box quality which made Tilli so resilient. And he did not realize that his British colleagues had also suffered privations and losses, that they were going out of their way to make him feel wanted and welcome with the small extras at their disposal. It was a tragic impasse, and from then on till his death in 1952 he withdrew more and more inside himself, and nothing would persuade him to leave Hamburg again except his duties inside Germany and the lure of his beloved Bavarian mountains.

Tilli's first husband, André Jolles, my natural father, died in February 1946. Since I did not know him, his death left no gap in my life. Only much later did we learn that his end was miserable, lonely and pathetic. In the Russian-occupied zone of Germany, he and his second family, having been members of the German National Socialist Party, were deprived of all but the barest necessi-ties of life. He died virtually of starvation. Emil Wolff's death was and is to me personally an irredeemable sadness, and to many still an irreplaceable loss. A friend and colleague of his who followed him as Rector of the University of Hamburg said of him : 'His spirit was so firmly rooted in the period of European enlighten-ment, especially in the eighteenth century, that one could regard him in his grandiose universality as a French encyclopaedist. He was a thorough classicist; an expert in Indo-Germanic philology; a mathematician and a philosopher; well versed in medicine, not to speak of his own special subject. Shoddiness and superficiality were anathema to him. He despised whatever shuns the clarity of day, could be sparklingly derisive and full of ironical wit. A plaster-cast of Houdon's Voltaire stood in a niche above his favourite chair and when the driving spirit of irony came over him, he looked remark-ably like the old wit of Ferney. Yet there was also a naïve kindness in him which made him so much like his favourite literary character, Uncle Toby in *Tristram Shandy*. All things coarse and mean were so foreign to him that they could not pollute him. But when he met with them his eyes would darken with sadness, even if he did not fully understand. Rarely if ever did he talk of what moved him most deeply. He followed Goethe's maxim : Judge what is recognizable and honour what is hidden. Speech to him was an attempt to clarify in words what perception made recognizable.'

After my journey to Hamburg in 1946 I thought it would take a hundred years to restore the town. Yet four years later, when I went to Tilli and Emil Wolff's Silver Wedding celebrations, enormous progress in rebuilding had already been made. Up to that time food and clothes parcels had been sent to friends and relations in Germany. Our own rationing system did not finish until 1954 and the time came when I received certain provisions from Germany. The boot was on the other foot. Tilli, ignoring all obstacles, started her round of visiting again as in pre-war days. She was still an inveterate traveller, although by then over seventy years old. Wherever she went she made friends and her travelling acquaintances were legion. People would write to her afterwards, gentlemen who had shared her compartment would take her out to lunch. Once, coming out of the station in Hamburg, she made for what she took to be a taxi, installed herself and her luggage and gave the address to which she wanted to be taken. The chauffeur helped her out and carried her suitcases to the front door. 'What do I owe you?' she asked. 'Nothing,' replied the gentleman, 'this is a private car, but it was a pleasure to convey such an intrepid lady.'

Her intrepidness received a very severe shock when Emil Wolff died in 1952, and later on that same year my husband Ifor. She suffered a stroke, but recovered almost completely. My second sister Jacoba had continued to live with them, and although tied by a large and growing general practice, she looked after them both, and after my stepfather's death remained with my mother till the end. The temperamental Maria, mentioned so often in Tilli's letters, also stayed, a trial and an enormous help to us all.

The latter years of Tilli's life were redeemed by her joy in her grandchildren. Despite the fact that hardly any of them spoke German, she made and retained contact with them by visits and letters and never forgot important dates. As they grew older she entered wholeheartedly into their plans and studies, their joys and disappointments. No one ever lacked the time or enthusiasm to go and see her.

Even towards the end of her life her weekly letters to me never stopped. In November 1957 she wrote : 'I have just listened to a late Beethoven quartet. It made me feel once again that this means

just everything to me, that it touches in an incomparable way the very depth of my soul. I am profoundly moved. The slow movement is of such quality that dying whilst listening to it would be easy. The clarity and beauty transcends all earthly misery, it lifts and guides one to celestial regions, right to the doors of heaven. Nothing heavy and ugly remains. Here is incomprehensible artistry, notes of strength and conviction, nothing mushy, only pure beauty.'
And during the same winter, 'When I think back on those horrible years of death and despair, caused by the satanic mania of a handful of people, I wonder that mankind and all the monstrously tortured natural elements did not revolt and shriek "Stop". When I said goodbye to Jella on Copenhagen station in 1939 and she whispered through her tears, "May God take care of you," I never thought we would survive the impending catastrophe. And yet mercifully we were preserved through times of death and tribulation. There must have been a reason behind this although it transcends comprehension. Why us, when thousands died and millions lost all their belongings? Perhaps there were still tasks we had to perform and it was ordained that we should meet again and our love would live. I am somehow convinced that those who were torn from the midst of their existence must have reached a stage of fulfilment, like in *The Bridge of San Luis Rey*. I don't suppose we had reached that stage.'

In her last letter to me, dictated to her nurse in October 1958 – she herself could not hold a pen, having suffered another stroke – she says : 'I have just listened on the radio to a lecture on World Peace. It was very illuminating, but now I am a little tired. When we next meet – soon my darling – I must tell you about it.'

We never met again. She deprived herself and all of us of the pleasure of a grand family reunion on her eightieth birthday. Mathilde Wolff-Mönckeberg died on 4 November, 1958.